CULINARY NOTEBOOKS

healthy desserts

fresh & fruity • cool & creamy • cakes & bakes

mc rae
PUBLISHING

This book was conceived,
edited and designed by
McRae Publishing Ltd
London

www.mcraebooks.com

NOTE TO OUR READERS
Eating eggs or egg whites that are not completely cooked poses the possibility of salmonella food poisoning. The risk is greater for pregnant women, the elderly, the very young, and persons with impaired immune systems. If you are concerned about salmonella, you can use reconstituted powdered egg whites or pasteurized eggs.

Culinary Notebooks series

Project Director Anne McRae
Art Director Marco Nardi

HEALTHY DESSERTS
Photography Brent Parker Jones
Text Carla Bardi
Editing Helen Cartwright
Food Styling Lee Blaylock
Food Styling Assistant Rochelle Seator
Prop Styling Lee Blaylock
Layouts Aurora Granata
Prepress Filippo Delle Monache

ISBN 978-88-6098-334-3

Printed in China

contents

getting started

There are 100 delicious—and healthy—dessert recipes in this book. Most are simple and quick to prepare. They are all rated for difficulty: 1 (simple), 2 (fairly simple), or 3 (challenging). The recipe selection includes low-fat, low-calorie, and gluten-free dishes, as well as many other recipes featuring healthy ingredients. In these two pages we have highlighted 25 of the most enticing recipes, just to get you started!

LOW-CALORIE

FRESH FRUIT SALAD with lemon syrup

FRESH FRUIT gazpacho

PEACH soup

LEMON SORBET with fresh berries

CHOCOLATE CHIP meringues

APPLE & BERRY cobbler

PINEAPPLE & ORANGE sorbet

LOW-FAT

LOW-FAT crème caramel

LOW-FAT ricotta cheesecake

LOW-FAT carrot cake

GLUTEN-FREE

GLUTEN-FREE almond shortbread

GLUTEN-FREE
chocolate roulade

GLUTEN-FREE
dried fruit balls

GLUTEN-FREE
chocolate cupcakes

GLUTEN-FREE
chocolate peanut cookies

STRAWBERRY
soup

RHUBARB POTS with
meringue topping

TUTTI FRUTTI
ice lollies

DAIRY-FREE
cupcakes

EDITOR'S CHOICE

GLUTEN-FREE chocolate layer cake

BEST LOW-CALORIE

RASPBERRY & LEMON
granita

BEST LOW-FAT

LOW-FAT
chocolate sorbet

BEST EGG-FREE

EGG-FREE
cupcakes

BEST GLUTEN-FREE

GLUTEN-FREE
almond torte with pears

BEST DIABETIC

DIABETIC
applesauce brownies

fresh & fruity

FRESH FRUIT gazpacho

- 4 cups (600 g) mixed berries, (raspberries, blackberries, and blueberries)
- 2 tablespoons sugar
- 4 ice cubes
- 1 cup (150 g) strawberries, hulled and sliced
- Freshly squeezed juice of $\frac{1}{2}$ lemon
- $\frac{1}{2}$ small ripe cantaloupe (rock) melon, peeled, seeded, and cut into cubes
- 2 large ripe peaches, pitted, peeled, and cut into cubes
- 2 tablespoons shredded (desiccated) coconut
- 8 wafer cookies, to serve
- 2 tablespoons confectioners' (icing) sugar, to dust

Serves 4 • Preparation 10 minutes • Difficulty 1

1. Put the mixed berries in a food processor. Add the sugar and ice cubes and blend until smooth. Press through a fine-mesh sieve into a bowl, discarding the seeds.
2. Drizzle the strawberries with the lemon juice.
3. Spoon the mixed berry purée into four serving bowls. Top with the strawberry mixture, melon, and peaches. Sprinkle with the coconut.
4. Dust the wafer cookies with the confectioners' sugar. Serve the gazpacho with the cookies on the side.

If you liked this recipe, you will love these as well.

BERRY FRUIT soup

PEACH soup

CANTALOUPE soup

This dessert soup is only good if made with locally grown, organic strawberries at the height of their spring-summer season. Don't even attempt to make it with frozen strawberries.

BERRY FRUIT soup

- 2 pounds (1 kg) fresh strawberries + 1 cup (150 g) extra, sliced, to serve
- 1/2 vanilla pod, split lengthwise
- 2 tablespoons sugar
- 1 tablespoon freshly squeezed lemon juice
- 1/3 cup (90 ml) freshly squeezed orange juice, strained
- 1/3 cup (90 ml) white grape juice
- 1/3 cup (90 ml) clear honey
- 2 tablespoons cornstarch (cornflour)
- 3 tablespoons cold water
- 4 tablespoons (60 ml) low-fat vanilla yogurt, to serve
- Mint leaves, to serve

Serves 6-8 • Preparation 15 minutes + 2 hours to chill • Cooking 5 minutes • Difficulty 1

1. Purée the strawberries in a food processor then press through a fine-mesh sieve into a bowl. Discard the seeds.
2. Scrape out the seeds from the vanilla pod and stir them into the strawberry purée along with the sugar and lemon juice.
3. Combine the orange juice, grape juice, and honey in a saucepan over medium heat and stir until the honey dissolves. Stir in the strawberry purée and bring to a gentle simmer. Mix the cornstarch and water in a small bowl until smooth. Pour into the soup. Stir until the soup thickens, then remove from the heat. Cool to room temperature. Chill in the refrigerator for at least 2 hours.
4. Divide the sliced strawberries among six to eight serving bowls or glasses. Ladle the fruit soup in over the top. Serve with a dollop of yogurt and decorate with mint leaves.

If you liked this recipe, you will love these as well.

FRESH FRUIT gazpacho

BLUEBERRY soup

STRAWBERRY soup

BLUEBERRY soup

Serves 4 • Preparation 15 minutes + 4 hours to chill
Cooking 2 minutes • Difficulty 1

- 1/2 cup (100 g) sugar
- Freshly squeezed juice of 1 orange
- 1 cup (250 ml) white grape juice
- 1 cup (250 ml) water
- 3 cups (450 g) fresh blueberries
- 8 tablespoons (120 ml) plain, low-fat yogurt

1. Bring the sugar, orange juice, grape juice, and water to a boil in a soup pot over medium heat. Simmer for 1 minute, stirring constantly. Add the blueberries and cook for 1 minute more. Remove from the heat and let cool completely.
2. Purée the mixture in a blender, then strain through a fine-mesh sieve into a bowl. Discard the solids. Cover the purée and chill for at least 4 hours.
3. Ladle the soup into four serving bowls, garnish each one with 2 tablespoons of yogurt, and serve.

PEACH soup

Serves 6–8 • Preparation 15 minutes + 2 hours to chill
Difficulty 1

- 3 pounds (1.5 kg) fresh peaches, peeled, pitted, and chopped
- 1 teaspoon ground ginger
- 1 cup (250 ml) low-fat plain or vanilla yogurt
- Fresh mint or basil leaves, to garnish

1. Set aside a few thin slices or tiny cubes of peach to garnish. Purée the remaining peaches and ginger in a food processor until smooth.
2. Stir in the yogurt. Cover and chill for at least 2 hours.
3. Ladle the soup into six to eight dessert glasses or bowls. Garnish with the reserved slices or cubes of peach and some fresh mint or basil leaves, and serve.

CANTALOUPE soup

Serves 4 • Preparation 10 minutes + 2 hours to chill
Difficulty 1

- 1 large cantaloupe (rock) melon, peeled, seeded, and cubed
- 1/4 cup (60 ml) dark rum
- 1/4 cup (60 ml) light (single) cream
- Finely grated zest from 1 unwaxed lemon
- 1/4 cup (60 ml) freshly squeezed orange juice

1. Reserve a few small cubes of the melon to garnish. Combine all the remaining ingredients in a food processor and purée until smooth. Strain through a fine-mesh sieve into a bowl. Discard the solids. Cover and chill the purée for 2 hours.
2. Ladle the soup into four serving glasses, garnish with the reserved melon, and serve.

STRAWBERRY soup

Serves 4–6 • Preparation 15 minutes + 2 hours to chill
Cooking 2 minutes • Difficulty 1

- 1 cup (250 ml) water
- 1 cup (250 ml) unsweetened apple juice
- 1/2 cup (100 g) sugar
- 1/2 teaspoon ground cinnamon
- 1/8 teaspoon ground cloves
- 3 cups (450 g) fresh strawberries + a few extra slices, to garnish
- 1 cup (250 ml) low-fat strawberry yogurt
- 2–3 drops red food coloring
- 1/4 cup (60 ml) low-fat sour cream

1. Combine 3/4 cup (180 ml) of water, the apple juice, sugar, cinnamon, and cloves in a medium soup pot. Bring to a boil, stirring occasionally. Remove from the heat.
2. Place the strawberries and remaining 1/4 cup (60 ml) of water in a blender. Process until smooth. Pour into the apple juice mixture. Stir in the yogurt and food coloring. Cover and refrigerate until well chilled, at least 2 hours.
3. Ladle the soup into four to six serving bowls. Drop a dollop of sour cream into the center of each bowl, garnish with a few slices of strawberries, and serve.

FRESH BERRIES with yogurt & toffee

- 1 cup (250 ml) plain, Greek-style yogurt
- ½ cup (100 g) superfine (caster) sugar
- 2 cups (300 g) strawberries, halved
- 1 cup (150 g) blueberries
- 1 cup (150 g) raspberries

Serves 4-6 • Preparation 15 minutes + 3 hours to chill • Cooking 8-10 minutes • Difficulty 1

1. Spoon the yogurt into a fine-mesh sieve. Cover the sieve and place over a bowl. Chill for 3 hours, until the yogurt has the same consistency as heavy (double) cream.
2. Put the sugar in a small, heavy-based saucepan over medium-low heat. Cook, tilting the pan back and forth and stirring with a metal spoon, until the sugar is dissolved and turns golden, 8–10 minutes.
3. Toss the strawberries, blueberries, and raspberries in a bowl. Spoon into four to six serving glasses or bowls. Top with a dollop of thickened yogurt, drizzle with the warm toffee syrup, and serve.

MELON BASKETS with lemon sorbet

2 small ripe cantaloupe (rock) melons, with unblemished skins
1 cup (150 g) strawberries, quartered
1 cup (150 g) blackberries
1 cup (150 g) raspberries
1 pound (500 g) lemon sorbet, storebought or homemade (see page 52)
Sprigs of fresh mint, to garnish

Serves 4 • Preparation 15 minutes • Difficulty 1

1. Cut the melons in half and discard the seeds. Scoop the flesh out of the melons using a melon baller and place in a bowl. Reserve the shells.
2. Add the strawberries, blackberries, and raspberries to the bowl with the melon and toss gently. Spoon the fruit into the reserved melon shells.
3. Use the melon baller to scoop out balls of lemon sorbet the same size as the melon balls. Add a few to each of the melon halves. Garnish with the mint and serve.

A mojito is a traditional Cuban cocktail, made with white rum, sugar, lime juice, and mint. This dessert includes all those traditional flavors, but adds lots of healthy, fresh fruit. If serving to children, or if you prefer not to serve alcohol, replace the rum with unsweetened white grape juice.

MOJITO fresh fruit salad

- 1 cup (150 g) cubed seeded watermelon
- 1 cup (150 g) seedless grapes
- 1 cup (150 g) cubed cantaloupe (rock) melon
- 1 cup (150 g) strawberries, hulled and quartered
- 2 kiwifruit, peeled and quartered
- 1 cup (150 g) blueberries
- 1 tablespoon fresh mint leaves
- 1 tablespoon sugar
- 3 tablespoons freshly squeezed lime juice
- 3 tablespoons white rum

Serves 4 • Preparation 15 minutes + 1 hour to chill • Difficulty 1

1. Combine the watermelon, grapes, cantaloupe, strawberries, kiwifruit, and blueberries in a salad bowl and toss gently.
2. Stir the mint, sugar, lime juice, and rum in a small bowl, crushing the mint with the back of a spoon while mixing to extract the flavor. Pour over the fruit mixture. Cover the bowl and chill for at least 1 hour.
3. Remove from the refrigerator, toss gently again, and serve.

If you liked this recipe, you will love these as well.

FRESH BERRIES with yogurt & toffee

MELON BASKETS with lemon sorbet

PINEAPPLE fresh fruit salad

SELFRIDGES

PINEAPPLE fresh fruit salad

- 1 pineapple
- 2 mangoes, peeled and diced
- 4 kiwifruit, peeled and diced
- 2 oranges, peeled and segmented
- 6 passionfruit, halved
- 1/3 cup (90 ml) orange liqueur, such as Cointreau
- 4 tablespoons confectioners' (icing) sugar
- 1 cup (150 g) raspberries
- 1 tablespoon coarsely chopped fresh mint leaves
- 1 cup (250 ml) low-fat vanilla yogurt, to serve

Serves 4-6 • Preparation 20 minutes + 2 hours to chill • Difficulty 1

1. Cut the pineapple in half lengthwise and, using a small sharp knife, make an incision around the perimeter 1 inch (2.5 cm) in from the skin on each half. Remove the flesh with a knife and spoon, leaving the shells intact. Slice the pineapple flesh into small pieces, discarding the tough core.
2. Put the pineapple flesh in a large bowl. Add the mangoes, kiwifruit, oranges, and passionfruit pulp, stirring to combine.
3. Mix the liqueur and confectioners' sugar in a small bowl and pour over the fruit. Add the raspberries and mint and stir gently to combine.
4. Spoon the fruit salad into the pineapple shells and refrigerate for 2 hours to allow the flavors to infuse. Serve with the yogurt passed separately.

WINTER fresh fruit salad

- 1 large pink grapefruit
- 3 navel oranges or a combination of navel oranges, blood oranges, mandarin oranges and/or tangerines
- 1/3 cup (90 ml) freshly squeezed lime or lemon juice
- 1/4 cup (60 ml) clear honey
- 1/4 teaspoon ground cardamom

Serves 4–6 • Preparation 15 minutes + 1 hour to chill • Cooking 5 minutes • Difficulty 1

1. Peel the citrus fruit. Cut away the membranes of the individual segments with a sharp knife and remove all the bitter white pith. Work over a small bowl to collect the juice. Put the fruit into another bowl.
2. Drain off any excess juice from the fruit into a small saucepan and add the juice from the small bowl. Add the lime or lemon juice, honey, and cardamom to the saucepan. Bring to a gentle boil, then simmer over low heat for 5 minutes. Remove from the heat and let cool to room temperature.
3. Pour over the fruit mixture and stir gently. Chill for 1 hour before serving.

Many fruits, such as pineapples, mangoes, and bananas, are enveloped in their own protective skins that must be removed before serving. Others, especially berryfruit, have no skins and often contain traces of chemicals used by growers. When possible, buy organic berryfruit. If you can't always get it, be sure to rinse the berries very thoroughly before serving.

FRESH FRUIT SALAD with lemon syrup

- 1/3 cup (90 ml) freshly squeezed lemon juice
- 1/3 cup (90 ml) water
- 2 tablespoons sugar
- 2 bananas, sliced
- 1/2 small pineapple, peeled, cored, and cut into chunks
- 2 cups (300 g) strawberries, sliced
- 4 passionfruit
- 3 tablespoons shredded (desiccated) coconut

Serves 4 • Preparation 15 minutes + 1–2 hours to chill • Cooking 2 minutes • Difficulty 1

1. Combine the lemon juice, water, and sugar in a small saucepan. Bring to a boil, then simmer over low heat for 2 minutes. Remove from the heat and let cool to room temperature.
2. Combine the bananas, pineapple, and strawberries in a large bowl. Cut the passionfruit in half and use a teaspoon to scoop out the pulp. Add to the bowl. Drizzle with the syrup and toss gently.
3. Chill in the refrigerator for 1–2 hours. Sprinkle with the coconut just before serving.

If you liked this recipe, you will love these as well.

17
WINTER
fresh fruit salad

21
MIXED MELON SALAD
with ginger syrup

22
TROPICAL
fresh fruit salad

THREE FRUIT SALAD with honey

- 1 cantaloupe (rock) melon, peeled, seeded, and cut into small cubes
- 2 kiwifruit, peeled and sliced
- 1 cup (150 g) small seedless black grapes
- 3 tablespoons freshly squeezed lime juice
- 1 tablespoon clear honey
- 1/2 teaspoon ground cinnamon
- Lime zest, to garnish

Serves 4 • Preparation 15 minutes + 1 hour to chill • Difficulty 1

1. Combine the melon, kiwifruit, and grapes in a serving bowl.
2. Whisk the lime juice, honey, and cinnamon in a small bowl. Drizzle over the fruit and chill in the refrigerator for 1 hour.
3. Garnish the salad with the lime zest and serve.

MIXED MELON SALAD with ginger syrup

- 1 cup (250 ml) water
- 1/2 cup (100 g) sugar
- 2 tablespoons finely chopped fresh ginger
- 1/2 cup (25 g) coarsely chopped fresh mint
- 1/4 small watermelon, cut into chunks
- 1 small cantaloupe (rock) melon, peeled, seeded, and cut into small cubes
- 1 small honeydew melon, peeled, seeded, and cut into small cubes

Serves 4–6 • Preparation 15 minutes + 1½ hours to cool & chill • Cooking 5 minutes • Difficulty 1

1. Heat the water, sugar, and ginger in a small saucepan over medium heat and bring to a boil. Decrease the heat to low and simmer for 5 minutes, until the liquid has reduced to a thin syrup. Remove from the heat and set aside to cool, about 30 minutes.
2. Strain the syrup through a fine-mesh sieve into a bowl. Add the mint. Combine the watermelon, cantaloupe, and honeydew melons in a large serving bowl and drizzle with the mint and ginger syrup. Chill for 1 hour before serving.

TROPICAL fresh fruit salad

Serves 4–6 • Preparation 15 minutes + 1–2 hours to chill
Difficulty 1

Salad

- 2 kiwifruit, peeled and cut into chunks
- 1 small mango, peeled, pitted, and cut into chunks
- 1 small papaya, peeled, seeded, and cut into chunks
- $\frac{1}{2}$ small pineapple, peeled and cut into chunks
- 3 clementines, peeled and segmented
- 3 passionfruit, halved

Coulis

- 2 cups (300 g) raspberries
- $\frac{1}{4}$ cup (50 g) superfine (caster) sugar
- Finely grated zest of $\frac{1}{2}$ unwaxed orange

Salad

1. Combine the kiwifruit, mango, papaya, pineapple, and clementines in a large bowl. Scoop out the passionfruit pulp and add to the fruit.

Coulis

1. Mash the raspberries, sugar, and orange zest in a bowl with a fork. Press through a fine-mesh sieve into a bowl, discarding the seeds. Drizzle over the fruit and chill for 1–2 hours before serving.

MANGO & BERRY salad

Serves 4 • Preparation 15 minutes + 2 hours to chill
Difficulty 1

- 2 mangoes, peeled, pitted, and diced
- 2 cups (300 g) strawberries, sliced
- 2 cups (300 g) mixed berries (raspberries, blackberries, blueberries)
- 2 tablespoons superfine (caster) sugar
- 2 tablespoons freshly squeezed lemon or lime juice

1. Combine the mangoes and all the berries in a medium bowl. Sprinkle with the sugar and drizzle with the lemon or lime juice. Toss well.
2. Chill in the refrigerator for 2 hours before serving.

BERRY FRUIT salad

Serves 4–6 • Preparation 15 minutes + 2–3 hours to cool & chill • Cooking 1–2 minutes • Difficulty 1

- $1\frac{1}{4}$ cups (300 ml) dry white wine
- $\frac{1}{4}$ cup (50 g) superfine (caster) sugar
- 1 teaspoon finely grated unwaxed lemon zest
- 1 clove
- 2 cups (300 g) strawberries, sliced
- 2 cups (300 g) raspberries
- 1 cup (150 g) blackberries
- 1 cup (150 g) blackcurrants

1. Combine the wine, sugar, lemon zest, and clove in a small saucepan. Bring to a boil, then simmer until the sugar is dissolved, 1–2 minutes. Remove from the heat and let cool a little.
2. Combine the strawberries, raspberries, blackberries, and blackcurrants in a serving bowl. Pour the warm syrup over the top. Let cool to room temperature, about 1 hour.
3. Chill in the refrigerator for 1–2 hours. Remove the clove before serving.

FRUIT SALAD cups

Serves 6–8 • Preparation 20 minutes + 1–2 hours to chill
Difficulty 1

- 2 ripe peaches, pitted and sliced
- 8 ripe apricots, pitted and sliced
- 2 ripe nectarines, pitted and sliced
- 1 mango, peeled, pitted, and cut into small pieces
- 2 cups (300 g) cherries, pitted and halved
- 1 tablespoon superfine (caster) sugar
- $\frac{1}{4}$ cup (60 ml) sweet dessert wine
- 1 tablespoon finely chopped fresh mint, to garnish

1. Combine the peaches, apricots, nectarines, mango, and cherries in a large bowl.
2. Sprinkle the sugar over the fruit and drizzle with the wine. Chill in the refrigerator for 1–2 hours.
3. Spoon the fruit and juices into six to eight serving cups. Garnish with the mint and serve.

BAKED SUMMER fruit

- 4 peaches or nectarines, pitted and quartered
- 6 apricots, halved and pitted
- 1 (1-inch/2.5-cm) piece ginger, peeled and grated
- 7 tablespoons light brown sugar + more, as needed
- 3 large red plums, pitted and quartered
- 3 large yellow plums or 6 greengage plums, halved and pitted
- 1 cup (150 g) blueberries
- 1 cup (150 g) raspberries
- 1 cup (250 ml) low-fat vanilla or plain yogurt, to serve

Serves 4–6 • Preparation 25 minutes • Cooking 20–30 minutes • Difficulty 1

1. Preheat the oven to 350°F (180°C/gas 4). Set out a shallow baking dish, about 12 inches (30 cm) in diameter.
2. Arrange the peaches and apricots cut-side up in the dish. Sprinkle with the ginger and 2 tablespoons of the brown sugar. Add the red and yellow plums and stir in the blueberries. Sprinkle the remaining 5 tablespoons of sugar over the fruit.
3. Bake for 20–30 minutes, until the fruit is tender and the juices have run. Remove the dish from the oven and stir in the raspberries. Mix gently into the hot juices. Taste for sweetness and stir in more brown sugar if needed. Serve warm or at room temperature with the yogurt.

POACHED PEARS with saffron

- 4 cups (1 liter) white wine
- 2 cups (400 g) sugar
- 2 teaspoons saffron threads
- 1 vanilla pod, split lengthwise
- Zest and juice of 2 unwaxed oranges
- 6 pears, peeled
- Low-fat vanilla or plain yogurt, to serve (optional)

Serves 6 • Preparation 15 minutes + 15 minutes to cool • Cooking 35–40 minutes • Difficulty 2

1. Heat the wine, sugar, saffron, vanilla pod, and orange zest and juice together in a large saucepan over medium-high heat until it reaches boiling point. Decrease the heat to low and simmer for 15 minutes.
2. Add the pears and cook just below the simmering point until the pears are tender, 20–25 minutes. Remove from the heat and let the pears cool in the syrup for 15 minutes.
3. Serve the pears warm with the yogurt, if desired.

Bananas are packed with nutrients. They are especially rich in potassium and vitamin B6 and are a good source of dietary fiber, vitamin C, and other B vitamins. They are believed to help lower blood pressure and cholesterol and to soothe the gastrointestinal tract, making them an ideal food for suffers of IBS.

If you prefer not to serve alcohol, replace the rum in this recipe with unsweetened apple juice.

CARAMELIZED bananas

- 1 tablespoon salted butter
- $1\frac{1}{2}$ tablespoons walnut oil
- 2 tablespoons clear honey
- 2 tablespoons firmly packed dark brown sugar
- 3 tablespoons skimmed milk
- 1 tablespoon dark raisins or golden raisins (sultanas)
- 4 firm, ripe bananas, about 1 pound (500 g) total weight, peeled, cut in half, and then sliced lengthwise
- 2 tablespoons dark rum or apple juice

Serves 4–6 • Preparation 15 minutes + $1\frac{1}{2}$ hours to cool & chill
Cooking 5–10 minutes • Difficulty 2

1. Melt the butter in a small saucepan over medium heat. Whisk in 1 tablespoon of walnut oil, the honey, and brown sugar. Stir until the sugar is dissolved. Add the milk and simmer, stirring constantly, until the sauce thickens slightly, 2–3 minutes. Remove from the heat and stir in the raisins. Set aside and keep warm.
2. Brush a large frying pan with the remaining walnut oil and place over high heat. Add the bananas and sauté until they begin to brown, 3–4 minutes. Set the bananas aside.
3. Add the rum to the pan, bring to a boil and deglaze, stirring with a wooden spoon to scrape up any browned bits from the pan. Simmer until reduced by half, about 30 seconds. Add the bananas and sauce to the pan and warm gently.
4. Divide the bananas among four to six bowls. Drizzle with the sauce and serve warm.

If you liked this recipe, you will love these as well.

BAKED SUMMER fruit

POACHED PEARS with chocolate

PINEAPPLE flambé

APPLE & RHUBARB crisp

Filling

- 3 apples, peeled, cored, and diced
- 2 tablespoons water
- 3 tablespoons sugar
- 1 pound (500 g) rhubarb, trimmed and cut into short lengths

Topping

- 1/2 cup (100 g) granola (muesli)
- 1/3 cup (50 g) self-rising flour
- 1/4 cup (50 g) firmly packed dark brown sugar
- 1/4 cup (60 g) salted butter, softened

Serves 4 • Preparation 15 minutes • Cooking 25–30 minutes • Difficulty 1

Filling

1. Preheat the oven to 400°F (200°C/gas 6). Lightly oil four 1-cup (250-ml) ramekins or mini soufflé dishes. Arrange on a baking sheet.
2. Mix the apples, water, and sugar in a large saucepan. Bring to a boil. Cover and simmer over low heat for 3 minutes. Stir in the rhubarb. Simmer until the rhubarb is beginning to soften, 10–15 minutes.

Topping

1. Mix the granola, flour, brown sugar, and butter in a small bowl. Spoon the fruit into the prepared ramekins. Sprinkle the topping evenly over the tops. Bake for 15 minutes, until crisp and golden. Serve warm.

APPLE & BERRY cobbler

Filling

- 1 cup (150 g) raspberries
- 1 cup (150 g) blueberries
- 2 apples, peeled, cored, and diced
- 2 tablespoons dark brown sugar
- $\frac{1}{2}$ teaspoon ground cinnamon
- 1 teaspoon finely grated unwaxed lemon zest
- 1 tablespoon freshly squeezed lemon juice
- $1\frac{1}{2}$ tablespoons cornstarch (cornflour)

Topping

- 1 large egg white
- $\frac{1}{4}$ cup (60 ml) soy milk
- $\frac{1}{4}$ teaspoon salt
- $\frac{1}{2}$ teaspoon vanilla extract (essence)
- 2 tablespoons dark brown sugar
- $\frac{3}{4}$ cup (120 g) whole-wheat (wholemeal) flour

Serves 6 • Preparation 20 minutes • Cooking 30–40 minutes
Difficulty 1

Filling

1. Preheat the oven to 350°F (180°C/gas 4). Lightly oil six $\frac{3}{4}$-cup (180-ml) ramekins or mini soufflé dishes.
2. Combine the raspberries, blueberries, apples, brown sugar, cinnamon, lemon zest, and lemon juice in a medium bowl. Stir in the cornstarch. Set aside.

Topping

1. Whisk the egg white in a small bowl until lightly beaten. Stir in the soy milk, salt, vanilla, brown sugar, and flour.
2. Divide the fruit filling evenly among the prepared ramekins. Spoon some topping over each one. Arrange on a baking sheet.
3. Bake for 30–40 minutes, until the berries are bubbling and juicy and the topping is golden brown. Serve warm.

These attractive little puddings make a perfect family dessert. Rhubarb is a healthy food with a low calorie count and plenty of dietary fiber, vitamins A and C, and potassium. Many believe that it helps protect against cancer, while lowering cholesterol and blood pressure. It can be quite acidic, which is why the sweet meringue topping on these desserts is so perfect.

RHUBARB POTS with meringue topping

Filling

1 pound (500 g) rhubarb, trimmed and cut into short lengths
1/4 cup (50 g) sugar
Finely grated zest of 1 unwaxed orange
2–3 tablespoons strawberry preserves (jam)
2 large egg yolks

Topping

2 large egg whites
1/4 cup (50 g) sugar

Serves 4 • Preparation 30 minutes • Cooking 55–65 minutes
Difficulty 2

Filling

1. Preheat the oven to 350°F (180°C/gas 4). Lightly oil four 3/4-cup (180-ml) ramekins or mini souffle dishes. Put the rhubarb in an ovenproof dish, sprinkle with the sugar and orange zest and stir gently. Cover and bake for 35–40 minutes, until tender.
2. Remove from the oven. Stir in the strawberry preserves and the egg yolks. Divide the mixture among the prepared ramekins. Place on a baking sheet and bake for 10 minutes.

Topping

1. Beat the egg whites until soft peaks form. Gradually beat in the sugar until stiff peaks form. Increase the oven temperature to 400°F (200°C/gas 6).
2. Spoon the meringue over the rhubarb in the ramekins to cover. Return to the oven for 10–15 minutes, until the meringue is puffy and golden. Serve warm.

If you liked this recipe, you will love these as well.

28
APPLE & RHUBARB crisp

29
APPLE & BERRY cobbler

38
LOW FAT PEACH crisp

POACHED PEARS with chocolate

- 1 (2-inch/5 cm) piece fresh ginger, peeled and thinly sliced
- ½ cup (120 ml) clear honey
- 8 cups (2 liters) water
- 4 firm, ripe pears
- 4 ounces (120 g) dark chocolate

Serves 4 • Preparation 15 minutes + time to cool • Cooking 10–15 minutes • Difficulty 1

1. Combine the ginger, honey, and water in a medium saucepan over high heat and bring to a boil. Reduce the heat to medium-low and simmer for 5 minutes.
2. Peel the pears and cut them half. Remove the cores. Gently lower the pears into the pan. Simmer until tender, 10–15 minutes (depending on how ripe they are). Let cool to room temperature in the poaching liquid.
3. Melt the chocolate in a double boiler over barely simmering water. Scoop the pears out of the poaching liquid and place in serving dishes. Drizzle with the chocolate and serve.

PINEAPPLE flambé

- 1 tablespoon butter
- 1 large ripe pineapple, peeled, cored, and cut into rings
- 4–6 cloves
- 1/4 cup (50 g) sugar
- 6 tablespoons (90 ml) brandy

Serves 6 • Preparation 15 minutes • Cooking 10 minutes • Difficulty 1

1. Melt the butter in a large frying pan over medium heat. Add the pineapple, cloves, and sugar. Sauté for 2–3 minutes, turning the pineapple carefully, until lightly browned on both sides.
2. Add 3 tablespoons of brandy and simmer until it evaporates. Add the remaining 3 tablespoons of brandy and light it with a match. When the flames have gone out, transfer the pineapple to serving plates, drizzle with the sauce, and serve.

Pears are a healthy food choice. They are an excellent source of dietary fiber, which helps to keep your intestines healthy and to lower cholesterol. Pears also contain useful amounts of vitamins B2, C, and E, as well as copper and potassium.

BAKED PEARS with ricotta & amaretti topping

- 4 firm, ripe organic pears, halved
- 1/2 cup (120 g) ricotta cheese
- 1/2 teaspoon cinnamon
- 4 tablespoons (60 ml) clear honey
- 12 Italian amaretti cookies, crushed

Serves 4 • Preparation 20 minutes • Cooking 20–25 minutes
Difficulty 1

1. Preheat the oven to 375°F (190°C/gas 5). Place the pears in a large shallow baking dish. Use a teaspoon to scoop out the cores, leaving a hollow in the center of each pear. Put 1–2 heaped teaspoons of ricotta in each pear. Dust with the cinnamon and drizzle with the honey.
2. Bake the pears for 10 minutes.
3. Remove from the oven. Sprinkle with the cookie crumbs. Bake for 10–15 more minutes, until the pears are soft and the topping is golden brown. Serve warm.

If you liked this recipe, you will love these as well.

25
POACHED PEARS with saffron

32
POACHED PEARS with chocolate

86
GLUTEN-FREE almond torte with pears

LOW-FAT apple & blueberry cobbler

Serves 4 • Preparation 30 minutes • Cooking 25–30 minutes • Difficulty 1

Filling

- 2 large apples, peeled, cored and thinly sliced
- 1 tablespoon freshly squeezed lemon juice
- 2 tablespoons light brown sugar
- 2 tablespoons cornstarch (cornflour)
- 1 teaspoon ground cinnamon
- 2 cups (300 g) blueberries

Topping

- 3/4 cup (120 g) all-purpose (plain) flour
- 3/4 cup (120 g) whole-wheat (wholemeal) flour
- 2 tablespoons light brown sugar
- 1 1/2 teaspoons baking powder
- 1/4 teaspoon salt
- 4 tablespoons (60 ml) canola oil
- 1/2 cup (120 ml) fat-free milk
- 1 teaspoon vanilla extract (essence)

Filling

1. Preheat the oven to 400°F (200°C/gas 6). Lightly oil a medium oval baking dish. Put the apples in a bowl and drizzle with the lemon juice.
2. Mix the brown sugar, cornstarch, and cinnamon in a small bowl. Add to the apples. Stir in the blueberries. Spoon into the prepared baking dish.

Topping

1. Combine both flours, the sugar, baking powder, and salt in a bowl. Add the oil and stir until the mixture resembles coarse crumbs. Stir in the milk and vanilla.
2. Turn the dough out onto a floured surface and knead until smooth. Roll into a rectangle about 1/2-inch (1-cm) thick. Use cookie cutters to cut out shapes. Re-roll the scraps and keep cutting out shapes until all the dough is used.
3. Place the dough "cookies" over the filling in the pan. Bake for 25–30 minutes, until the apples are tender and the topping is golden brown. Serve warm.

LOW-FAT grape & almond clafoutis

- 2 pounds (1 kg) seedless white grapes
- 4 large eggs
- 1/2 cup (75 g) finely ground almonds
- 1 1/4 cups (300 ml) light (single) cream
- 2/3 cup (150 ml) skimmed milk
- 3 tablespoons sugar
- 1 teaspoon vanilla extract (essence)
- 1 cup (250 ml) fat-free vanilla or plain yogurt, to serve (optional)

Serves 6-8 • Preparation 15 minutes • Cooking 30-35 minutes
Difficulty 1

1. Preheat the oven to 350°F (180°C/gas 4). Lightly oil a medium oval baking dish. Put the grapes in the dish.
2. Whisk the eggs, almonds, cream, milk, sugar, and vanilla in a bowl until well mixed. Pour over the grapes.
3. Bake for 30–35 minutes, until set and golden brown. Serve warm, with the yogurt, if desired.

Peaches are low in calories and fat, and sweetened with their own natural sugars, such as sucrose, fructose, and glucose. They are a good source of potassium, carotenes, and flavonoids. Many believe that regular consumption of peaches can help protect against heart disease and cancer.

LOW-FAT peach crisp

- 8 ripe yellow peaches, peeled, pitted and sliced
- Freshly squeezed juice of 1 lemon
- $^{1}/_{2}$ cup (75 g) whole-wheat (wholemeal) flour
- $^{1}/_{3}$ cup (50 g) old-fashioned (quick-cooking) oats
- $^{1}/_{4}$ cup (50 g) firmly packed dark brown sugar
- $^{1}/_{2}$ teaspoon ground cinnamon
- $^{1}/_{4}$ teaspoon ground nutmeg
- 3 tablespoons salted butter
- 1 cup (250 ml) fat-free vanilla or plain yogurt, to serve (optional)

Serves 6 • Preparation 15 minutes • Cooking 20–30 minutes
Difficulty I

1. Preheat the oven to 375°F (190°C/gas 5). Lightly oil a 10-inch (25-cm) pie pan.
2. Arrange the peach slices in the prepared pan. Drizzle with the lemon juice.
3. Combine the flour, oats, brown sugar, cinnamon, and nutmeg in a small bowl. Add the butter, rubbing it in with your fingers. Sprinkle the mixture over the peaches.
4. Bake for 20–30 minutes, until the peaches are tender and the topping is browned. Serve warm, with the yogurt, if desired.

If you liked this recipe, you will love these as well.

37
LOW-FAT
grape & almond clafoutis

40
LOW-FAT
apple crisp

45
LOW-FAT
plum tart

LOW-FAT apple crisp

Filling

4	large Granny Smith apples, peeled, cored, sliced
1	teaspoon pumpkin pie spice (allspice)

Topping

1	cup (150 g) old-fashioned (quick-cooking) oats
$^1/_3$	cup (50 g) oat bran
$^1/_3$	cup (50 g) whole-wheat (wholemeal) flour
2	tablespoons dark brown sugar
1	teaspoon ground cinnamon
$^1/_4$	cup (60 ml) hazelnut oil
2	tablespoons slivered almonds

Serves 4-6 • Preparation 20 minutes • Cooking 45 minutes • Difficulty 1

Filling

1. Preheat the oven to 350°F (180°C/gas 4).
2. Mix the apples with the spice and place into a 9-inch (23-cm) baking dish. Cover with aluminum foil and bake for 15 minutes.

Topping

1. Combine the oats, oat bran, flour, brown sugar, cinnamon, and oil in the bowl of a food processor and process until crumbly. Stir in the almonds.
2. Spoon the topping over the apples, pressing firmly with the back of the spoon. Bake for 30 minutes, until the apples are tender and the topping is golden. Serve warm.

LOW-FAT apple brown betty

Filling

- 5 Golden Delicious apples, peeled and thinly sliced
- 1 cup (250 ml) apple cider
- $^{1}/_{2}$ teaspoon ground cinnamon
- 1 teaspoon vanilla extract (essence)
- 1 tablespoon salted butter

Topping

- 3 slices whole-wheat (wholemeal) bread, cut into cubes
- 1 tablespoon salted butter
- 3 tablespoons walnuts, chopped
- 2 tablespoons dark brown sugar
- $^{1}/_{2}$ teaspoon ground cinnamon

Serves 4–6 • Preparation 20 minutes • Cooking 40 minutes • Difficulty 1

Filling

1. Preheat the oven to 350°F (180°C/gas 4).
2. Place all the filling ingredients in a saucepan over medium heat and cook, stirring occasionally, until the apples are softened but still hold their shape, about 10 minutes.

Topping

1. Put the bread in a food processor and pulse until it forms coarse crumbs. Place in a bowl. Melt the butter and pour over the bread crumbs. Add the walnuts, brown sugar, and cinnamon and mix well.
2. Transfer the filling mixture to a 9-inch (23-cm) pie dish and sprinkle with the topping. Bake for 30 minutes, until golden brown. Serve warm.

Apples are a good source of vitamin C, pectin, dietary fiber, and potassium. Since many of their most beneficial nutritional properties are contained in the skins, they are best served peel on. However, commercially grown apples are often sprayed with harmful chemicals, so be sure to buy organic apples, peel them, or rinse very thoroughly before serving.

BAKED APPLES with low-fat streusel topping

- 4 large organic baking apples
- 1/4 cup (50 g) firmly packed dark brown sugar
- 1/4 cup (30 g) old-fashioned (quick-cooking) oats
- 2 tablespoons chopped dates
- 1/2 teaspoon ground cinnamon
- 1/2 teaspoon ground ginger
- 4 teaspoons salted butter

Serves 4 • Preparation 15 minutes • Cooking 45–50 minutes • Difficulty 1

1. Preheat the oven to 350°F (180°C/gas 4). Core the apples, cutting out a 1-inch (2.5-cm) cylinder from the center of each, almost but not all the way through to the bottom. Arrange the apples in a shallow baking dish in which they fit snuggly, one against the other.
2. Combine the brown sugar, oats, dates, cinnamon, and ginger in a small bowl. Stuff each apple with this mixture. It will not all fit, and should spill over the tops of the apples. Place 1 teaspoon of butter on top of each apple.
3. Bake for 45–50 minutes, until the apples are softened. Spoon the cooking liquid from the baking dish over the apples and serve warm.

If you liked this recipe, you will love these as well.

LOW-FAT apple & blueberry cobbler

LOW-FAT apple brown betty

LOW-FAT apple strudel

LOW-FAT apple strudel

- $1\frac{1}{2}$ pounds (750 g) Granny Smith apples, peeled, cored, and sliced
- 1 tablespoon sugar
- $\frac{1}{2}$ teaspoon ground cinnamon
- 2 tablespoons cold water
- 8 sheets filo (phyllo) pastry
- Olive oil spray
- 4 tablespoons fine dry bread crumbs
- Confectioners' (icing sugar), to dust
- $\frac{3}{4}$ cup (180 ml) low-fat vanilla yogurt, to serve

Serves 4–6 • Preparation 20 minutes • Cooking 40 minutes
Difficulty 2

1. Preheat the oven to 375°F (190°C/gas 5). Line a large baking sheet with parchment paper. Combine the apples, sugar, cinnamon, and water in a large frying pan. Simmer over medium-low heat until tender, about 10 minutes. Let cool while you prepare the pastry.
2. Place a sheet of filo on a work surface. Spray with oil. Sprinkle with bread crumbs. Top with another filo sheet, spray with oil and sprinkle with bread crumbs. Repeat with the remaining filo, oil, and bread crumbs, finishing with a layer of filo.
3. Arrange the apple mixture down one long side of the pastry, 3 inches (8 cm) in from the edge and leaving a 1-inch (2.5-cm) border at the short ends. Fold the short ends in and roll up to enclose the filling. Transfer to the prepared baking sheet, seam-side down. Spray with oil.
4. Bake for 30 minutes, until golden brown. Dust with confectioners' sugar, and serve warm with the yogurt.

LOW-FAT plum tart

- 2/3 cup (100 g) whole-wheat (wholemeal) flour
- 1/3 cup (50 g) all-purpose (plain) flour
- 2 tablespoons walnut or canola oil
- 1 tablespoon unsalted butter
- 1 tablespoon sugar
- 1/8 teaspoon salt
- 1 tablespoon iced water
- 1/4 cup (50 g) firmly packed dark brown sugar
- 1 tablespoon wheat germ
- 6 large red plums, about 1 pound (500 g) total weight, pitted and thinly sliced
- 2 tablespoons seedless raspberry preserves (jam), warmed

Serves 4–6 • Preparation 20 minutes + 30 minutes to chill • Cooking 45–50 minutes • Difficulty 2

1. Preheat the oven to 400°F (200°C/gas 6). Combine both flours, the oil, butter, sugar, and salt in a bowl. Beat until the mixture resembles bread crumbs. Add the water and stir until it comes together as a dough. Shape into a disk and wrap in plastic wrap (cling film). Chill for 30 minutes.
2. Roll out the dough and place in an 8-inch (20-cm) round tart pan with a removable bottom. Trim the edges even with the rim and set aside. Put the scraps of dough in a bowl and rub in the brown sugar and wheat germ.
3. Arrange the plums in the tart shell. Brush with the preserves and sprinkle with the wheat germ mixture.
4. Bake for 45–50 minutes, until the plums are tender and bubbling and the topping is lightly browned. Serve warm.

cool & creamy

LOW-FAT panna cotta with passionfruit

- 1 cup (250 ml) semi-skimmed milk
- 2 cinnamon sticks
- 2 cups (500 ml) low-fat vanilla yogurt
- $\frac{1}{4}$ cup (60 ml) boiling water
- 1 tablespoon unflavored gelatin
- 2 passionfruit, halved

Serves 4 • Preparation 15 minutes + 6 hours to chill • Cooking 5 minutes • Difficulty 2

1. Bring the milk and cinnamon sticks to a boil in a small saucepan over medium heat. Remove from the heat and let cool to room temperature. Remove the cinnamon sticks.
2. Combine the flavored milk and yogurt in a large bowl. Put the boiling water in a cup and sprinkle with the gelatin. Whisk with a fork until the gelatin is dissolved. Stir into the yogurt mixture until smooth.
3. Divide the yogurt mixture among four $\frac{3}{4}$-cup (180-ml) ramekins. Place on a large plate and cover with plastic wrap (cling film). Chill for 6 hours, until firm.
4. Carefully run a round-bladed knife around the edge of each ramekin. Turn the panna cotta out onto serving plates. Scoop the passionfruit pulp out of the fruit with a teaspoon and spoon evenly over the panna cotta. Serve.

If you liked this recipe, you will love these as well.

78

LOW-FAT
crème caramel

80

LOW-FAT
crème brûlée

81

LOW-FAT
vanilla custards

High-quality dark chocolate contains substances that are believed to be good for your cardio-vascular system. Choose dark (semisweet, bittersweet) chocolate with at least 70% cocoa solids. Avoid products made with hydrogenated fats or those labelled "chocolate-flavored," as these are not good for your health. Remember that all the beneficial nutrients have been removed from white chocolate, so it is not a healthful food.

LOW-FAT chocolate sorbet

- $2^1/_2$ cups (620 ml) water
- $^1/_2$ cup (75 g) unsweetened cocoa powder
- 1 cup (200 g) sugar
- 3 ounces (90 g) high-quality dark chocolate, finely chopped
- 2 teaspoons vanilla extract (essence)
- Low-fat ice cream wafers or cookies, to serve

Serves 4–6 • Preparation 15 minutes + 30 minutes to chill & time to churn • Cooking 5 minutes • Difficulty 2

1. Bring the water to a boil in a medium saucepan over high heat. Place the cocoa in a cup and stir in 2–3 tablespoons of boiling water until smooth. Stir the sugar and cocoa mixture into the water, decrease the heat to low, and simmer for 5 minutes, stirring frequently.
2. Remove from the heat. Add the chocolate and vanilla, stirring until the chocolate melts. Cover, let cool to room temperature, then chill for 30 minutes.
3. Pour the chocolate mixture into an ice cream machine and freeze according to the manufacturer's instructions.
4. Scoop the sorbet into dessert glasses or bowls and serve with the wafers or cookies

If you liked this recipe, you will love these as well.

LOW-FAT CHOCOLATE mousse

LOW-FAT CHOCOLATE pudding

CHOCOLATE AVOCADO puddings

SELFRIDGES

LOW-FAT yogurt & almond ice cream

- 2 cups (500 ml) fat-free plain yogurt
- 1 cup (250 ml) low-fat vanilla soy milk, chilled
- $^1/_3$ cup (90 ml) clear honey
- 1 tablespoon canola oil
- $^1/_2$ teaspoon almond extract (essence)
- $^1/_4$ cup (30 g) coarsely chopped almonds
- 1 tablespoon slivered almonds, to serve

Serves 4-6 • Preparation 10 minutes + time to churn • Difficulty 1

1. Whisk the yogurt, soy milk, honey, oil, and almond extract in a bowl until well blended. Pour the mixture into an ice cream machine and freeze according to the manufacturer's instructions. Add the coarsely chopped almonds 1–2 minutes before the machine finishes churning.
2. Scoop into serving glasses or bowls, sprinkle with the slivered almonds, and serve.

LOW-FAT vanilla ice cream

- 1½ teaspoons unflavored gelatin
- 2 tablespoons water
- 3 cups (750 ml) skimmed milk, divided
- 1 vanilla bean
- 3 large egg yolks
- 1 (14-ounce/400-g) can nonfat sweetened condensed milk
- Unsweetened cocoa powder, to dust

Serves 6 • Preparation 15 minutes + 1 hour to chill & time to churn
Cooking 10 minutes • Difficulty 2

1. Sprinkle the gelatin over the water in a cup. Set aside. Pour 1½ cups (375 ml) of milk into a large saucepan. Scrape the vanilla seeds into the milk and add the pod. Heat over medium heat until almost boiling.
2. Whisk the egg yolks and condensed milk in a bowl. Pour in the hot milk, whisking until blended. Return to the pan and stir over medium heat until the back of the spoon is lightly coated, 3–5 minutes. Do not allow the mixture to boil.
3. Strain the custard through a fine-mesh sieve into a large bowl. Whisk in the gelatin mixture until dissolved. Whisk in the remaining 1½ cups (375 ml) of milk. Chill for 1 hour.
4. Pour the mixture into an ice cream machine and freeze according to the manufacturer's instructions. Scoop into bowls, dust with cocoa, and serve.

Traditionally, a sorbet is made with a sugar syrup and fruit juice, wine, or liqueur and does not usually contain any milk or other dairy products. This means that a classic sorbet will always be low-fat or fat-free. However, this is not always so and some sorbets do contain dairy products. If you are following a low-fat diet, check labels if you are buying sorbet, and use low-fat versions of any dairy products in homemade sorbet recipes. Remember that sorbets often contain a lot of sugar so are not always recommended for weight loss.

LEMON SORBET with fresh berries

- Zest of 1 unwaxed lemon, very finely chopped + extra strips of zest, to garnish
- 1 cup (250 ml) cold water
- 1/2 cup (100 g) sugar
- 1/2 cup (120 ml) freshly squeezed lemon juice
- 1/2 cup (120 ml) sparkling (carbonated) mineral water
- Fresh berries, to serve

Serves 4 • Preparation 15 minutes + time to cool & churn • Cooking 5 minutes • Difficulty 2

1. Stir the finely chopped lemon zest, water, and sugar in a medium saucepan over high heat. Bring to a boil, then decrease the heat to medium and simmer for 5 minutes. Remove from the heat and let cool.
2. Stir the lemon syrup, lemon juice, and mineral water in a bowl. Pour into an ice cream machine and freeze according to the manufacturer's instructions.
3. Scoop the sorbet into dessert glasses or bowls, sprinkle with the berries, garnish with the strips of zest, and serve.

If you liked this recipe, you will love these as well.

STRAWBERRY sorbet

PEACH sorbet

PINEAPPLE & ORANGE sorbet

COFFEE frozen yogurt

Serves 4 • Preparation 10 minutes • Difficulty 1

- 2 cups (500 g) low-fat vanilla frozen yogurt
- 2 tablespoons Kahlua or other coffee liqueur
- 8 tablespoons (120 ml) hot espresso coffee

1. Scoop the frozen yogurt into four small espresso coffee cups.
2. Stir the coffee liqueur into the coffee, drizzle over the frozen yogurt in the cups, and serve.

STRAWBERRY sorbet

Serves 4 • Preparation 10 minutes + 30 minutes to cool & time to churn • Cooking 2–3 minutes • Difficulty 1

- 1/2 cup (100 g) sugar
- 2 cups (500 ml) water
- 3 cups (450 g) ripe strawberries, chopped
- 1 1/4 cups (300 g) low-fat plain yogurt

1. Put the sugar and water in a medium saucepan over medium heat. Bring to a boil and simmer, stirring constantly, until the sugar has completely dissolved, 2–3 minutes. Remove from the heat and set aside to cool, about 30 minutes.
2. Add the strawberries to the cooled sugar syrup. Stir in the yogurt then chop the mixture in a food processor until smooth.
3. Transfer to an ice cream machine and freeze according to the manufacturer's instructions.
4. Scoop into serving glasses or bowls and serve.

PEACH sorbet

Serves 6–8 • Preparation 15 minutes + 30 minutes to cool & time to churn • Cooking 2–3 minutes • Difficulty 2

- 1 3/4 cups (350 g) sugar
- 1 1/2 cups (375 ml) water
- 1 1/2 pounds (750 g) ripe white peaches, peeled, pitted, and sliced
- Freshly squeezed juice of 2 lemons
- 1 large egg white

1. Combine the sugar and water in a medium saucepan over medium heat. Bring to a boil and simmer, stirring constantly, until the sugar has completely dissolved, 2–3 minutes. Remove from the heat and set aside to cool, about 30 minutes.
2. Chop the peaches in a food processor until smooth. You should have just over 1 pound (500 g) of peach purée. Stir the peach purée and lemon juice into the cooled sugar syrup.
3. Beat the egg white with an electric mixer on high speed until stiff. Fold into the peach mixture. Transfer to an ice cream machine and freeze according to the manufacturer's instructions.
4. Scoop the sorbet into serving glasses or bowls, and serve.

GRAPEFRUIT granita

Serves 6 • Preparation 20 minutes + time to cool & freeze Cooking 2–3 minutes • Difficulty 2

- 3/4 cup (150 g) sugar
- 1/4 cup (60 ml) water
- 2 cups (500 ml) freshly squeezed grapefruit juice
- 3/4 cup (180 ml) Campari

1. Combine the sugar and water in a small saucepan, bring to a boil, then remove from the heat.
2. Stir the grapefruit juice and Campari in a large bowl. Stir the sugar syrup into the grapefruit mixture and set aside to cool, about 30 minutes.
3. Pour into a shallow freezerproof container. Cover with plastic wrap (cling film). Freeze until almost solid, 1–2 hours. Use a fork or hand held beater to break up into large crystals. Replace in the freezer until almost frozen again, then break it up again with a fork. Repeat three or four times, until the crystals are separate and completely frozen.
4. Spoon into wine goblets or cups and serve.

3.

With fresh pineapple and orange juice, this sorbet is packed with vitamin C. Pineapple is also a good source of vitamins B1, B6, manganese, copper, magnesium, and dietary fiber and contains enzymes that aid in digestion and have anti-inflammatory effects that are believed to reduce swelling in conditions like arthritis, sinusitis, and sore throats.

PINEAPPLE & ORANGE sorbet

- 1/2 cup (100 g) sugar
- 1/2 cup (120 ml) water
- 1 small, sweet pineapple, peeled, cored, and cut into chunks
- 2 cups (500 ml) freshly squeezed orange juice
- 2 teaspoons finely grated unwaxed orange zest
- 1 tablespoon freshly squeezed lemon juice

Serves 4–6 • Preparation 15 minutes + 30 minutes to chill & time to churn • Cooking 5 minutes • Difficulty 2

1. Bring the sugar and water to a boil in a medium saucepan over medium-high heat, stirring gently until the sugar is completely dissolved. Remove from the heat.
2. Chop the pineapple in a food processor until smooth. Transfer to a metal bowl and stir in the sugar syrup, orange juice, orange zest, and lemon juice. Chill in the refrigerator for 30 minutes.
3. Pour into an ice cream machine and freeze according to the manufacturer's instructions.
4. Scoop the sorbet into dessert glasses or bowls and serve.

If you liked this recipe, you will love these as well.

LEMON SORBET with fresh berries

STRAWBERRY sorbet

MELON SORBET with basil

MELON SORBET with basil

- $1^1/_2$ pounds (750 g) cantaloupe (rock) melon flesh, peeled weight, cut in cubes
- 6 fresh basil leaves + extra, to garnish
- $^1/_3$ cup (90 ml) freshly squeezed orange juice
- $^3/_4$ cup (150 g) sugar
- $^1/_4$ teaspoon salt

Serves 6 • Preparation 15 minutes + 1 hour to chill & time to churn
Difficulty 1

1. Place 1 pound (500 g) of the melon cubes in a blender with the basil, orange juice, sugar, and salt. Chop until the sugar has dissolved and the mixture is smooth, about 30 seconds. Transfer to a bowl and chill for 1 hour.
2. Pour the mixture into an ice cream machine and freeze according to the manufacturer's instructions.
3. Spoon the remaining melon cubes into six serving bowls or glasses. Scoop the frozen sorbet over the top. Decorate with the extra basil and serve.

RASPBERRY & LEMON granita

- $\frac{3}{4}$ cup (150 g) sugar
- 1 tablespoon finely grated unwaxed lemon zest
- 3 cups (750 ml) water, divided
- 3 cups (450 g) raspberries
- $\frac{1}{2}$ cup (120 ml) freshly squeezed lemon juice

Serves 4–6 • Preparation 15 minutes + time to freeze • Cooking 2–3 minutes • Difficulty 2

1. Bring the sugar, lemon zest, and $1\frac{1}{2}$ cups (375 ml) of water to a boil in a medium saucepan over medium-high heat, stirring until the sugar is dissolved. Remove from the heat. Stir in the raspberries and let cool to room temperature.
2. Chop in a food processor until smooth. Press the purée through a fine-mesh sieve, discarding the seeds. Stir in the lemon juice and remaining $1\frac{1}{2}$ cups (375 ml) of water.
3. Pour into a shallow freezerproof container. Cover with plastic wrap (cling film). Freeze until almost solid, 1–2 hours. Use a fork or hand-held beater to break up into large crystals. Replace in the freezer until almost frozen again, then break it up again with a fork. Repeat three or four times, until the crystals are separate and completely frozen.
4. Spoon into wine goblets or bowls and serve.

Prepare these frozen fruit ice lollies as a healthy after-school snack or family dessert during the summer months.

TUTTI FRUTTI ice lollies

- 3 cups (450 g) fresh strawberries
- 6 tablespoons (90 ml) clear honey
- 3 large ripe yellow peaches, peeled, pitted, and sliced
- 5 large kiwifruit, peeled and sliced

Serves 8 • Preparation 30 minutes + 6 hours to freeze • Difficulty 2

1. Purée the strawberries with a hand-held blender. Press the purée through a fine-mesh sieve, discarding the seeds. Stir 2 tablespoons of honey into the purée. Pour the strawberry purée into eight ice lolly molds until each mold is one-third full. Freeze until firm, about 2 hours.
2. Purée the peaches with a hand-held blender. Press the purée through a fine-mesh sieve, discarding any solids. Stir 2 tablespoons of honey into the purée. Pour the peach purée into the eight ice lolly molds until each mold is two-thirds full. Freeze until firm, about 2 hours.
3. Purée the kiwifruit with a hand-held blender. Stir the remaining 2 tablespoons of honey into the purée. Pour the kiwifruit purée into the eight ice lolly molds until each mold is full. Freeze until firm, about 2 hours.

If you liked this recipe, you will love these as well.

PINEAPPLE & ORANGE sorbet

MELON SORBET with basil

RASPBERRY & LEMON granita

LEMON TOFU cream

- 1 tablespoon finely grated unwaxed lemon zest
- 1/4 cup (60 ml) freshly squeezed lemon juice
- 1/2 cup (120 ml) clear honey
- 12 ounces (350 g) silken tofu, firm or extra-firm, drained
- 1 cup (150 g) fresh raspberries

Serves 4 • Preparation 10 minutes • Difficulty 1

1. Combine the lemon zest, lemon juice, honey, and tofu in a blender and purée until smooth.
2. Divide the silky lemon cream evenly among four bowls or serving glasses. Garnish each portion with raspberries. Keep chilled until ready to serve.

BANANA mousse

- 1/4 cup (60 ml) semi-skimmed milk
- 4 teaspoons sugar
- 1 teaspoon vanilla extract (essence)
- 2 medium bananas
- 1 cup (250 ml) plain low-fat yogurt
- 15 fresh raspberries, to decorate

Serves 4 • Preparation 15 minutes + 2 hours to chill • Difficulty 1

1. Combine the milk, sugar, vanilla, and bananas in a blender. Process for 15 seconds at high speed until smooth.
2. Pour the mixture into a medium bowl. Fold in the yogurt.
3. Spoon into four dessert glasses, cover with plastic wrap (cling film), and chill for 2 hours. Decorate with the raspberries just before serving.

Cantaloupe melons, also known as rock melons, are very low in calories but packed with nutrients. They are an excellent source of carotenes, vitamins B6 and C, and potassium, and a good source of vitamins B1 (thiamine), B3 (niacin), and B5 (pantothenic acid), as well as dietary fiber and folic acid.

MELON fool

- 1 cup (250 ml) low-fat lemon yogurt
- 1 cup (250 ml) fat-free plain yogurt
- $^1/_4$ cup (60 ml) water
- $^1/_4$ cup (60 ml) freshly squeezed lemon juice
- Zest of 1 unwaxed lemon, removed in wide strips
- 2 tablespoons sugar
- 4 fresh mint leaves + extra, to garnish
- 2 tablespoons cream cheese
- 1 small cantaloupe (rock) melon, about $1^1/_2$ pounds (750 g), peeled, seeded, and cut into chunks + a few small cubes, to garnish
- 1 small honeydew melon, about 1 pound (500 g), peeled, seeded, and cut into chunks + a few small cubes, to garnish

Serves 6 • Preparation 15 minutes + 12 hours to drain + 1 hour to stand & chill • Cooking 10 minutes • Difficulty 2

1. Set a fine-mesh sieve over a bowl. Carefully spoon both yogurts into the sieve. Place in the refrigerator to drain overnight. Discard the liquid in the bowl, and spoon the yogurt cheese in the sieve into a container with a tight-fitting lid. Chill until ready to use.
2. Combine the water, lemon juice and zest, sugar, and mint in a medium saucepan and bring to a boil over medium-high heat. Remove from the heat and let stand for 30 minutes. Discard the mint and lemon zest. Place over high heat and boil until reduced to 1 tablespoon, 3–4 minutes. Place in a small bowl, cover, and chill for 30 minutes.
3. Whisk the cream cheese and syrup into the yogurt cheese. Combine both melons in a blender and purée until smooth. Add the yogurt cheese and pulse a few times to blend.
4. Divide the mixture evenly among six champagne flutes. Garnish with the extra melon and mint leaves, and serve.

If you liked this recipe, you will love these as well.

LEMON TOFU cream

BANANA mousse

FAST fruit parfait

LOW-FAT chocolate mousse

- 3 ounces (90 g) dark chocolate, chopped
- 1 tablespoon unsweetened cocoa powder
- ½ teaspoon coffee granules
- ½ teaspoon vanilla extract (essence)
- 2 tablespoons boiling water
- 2 large egg whites
- 1 tablespoon superfine (caster) sugar
- ½ cup (120 ml) low-fat Greek-style yogurt
- 12 fresh raspberries, to decorate

Serves 4 • Preparation 15 minutes + 12 hours to chill • Cooking 5–10 minutes • Difficulty 1

1. Put the chocolate in the top of a double boiler. Mix the cocoa, coffee, and vanilla with the water, and add to the chocolate. Stir over barely simmering water until melted. Set aside to cool slightly.
2. Beat the egg whites in a bowl until soft peaks form, then beat in the sugar until thick and glossy. Beat the yogurt into the cooled chocolate. Fold one-third of the egg whites into the chocolate mixture, then fold in the remaining whites.
3. Spoon into four serving cups or glasses and chill overnight. Serve sprinkled with a few raspberries.

LOW-FAT chocolate pudding

- 2 1/4 cups (600 ml) skimmed milk, divided
- 3/4 cup (150 g) sugar, divided
- 1/8 teaspoon salt
- 2/3 cup (100 g) unsweetened cocoa powder
- 2 tablespoons cornstarch (cornflour)
- 1 large egg, lightly beaten
- 1 teaspoon vanilla extract (essence)

Serves 4 • Preparation 15 minutes • Cooking 10 minutes • Difficulty 2

1. Combine 1 1/2 cups (375 ml) milk and 1/3 cup (70 g) of sugar with the salt in a medium saucepan over medium heat and bring to a boil, stirring occasionally.
2. Mix the remaining sugar, cocoa, and cornstarch in a medium bowl. Whisk in the remaining milk. Whisk the hot milk mixture into the cocoa mixture. Pour the mixture back into the pan and bring to a simmer over medium heat, whisking constantly, until thickened and glossy, about 3 minutes. Remove from the heat.
3. Whisk 1 cup (250 ml) of the hot cocoa mixture into the beaten egg. Return the egg mixture to the pan and cook over medium-low heat, whisking constantly, until steaming and thickened, about 2 minutes. Do not let the mixture boil. Whisk in the vanilla and serve warm.

This eye-catching dessert is perfect if you are following a low-fat diet. It is also not very high in calories and contains all the goodness of the raspberries and yogurt.

RASPBERRY RIPPLE meringue desserts

- 4 large egg whites
- 3/4 cup (150 g) superfine (caster) sugar
- 1/2 teaspoon vanilla extract (essence)
- 2 cups (300 g) raspberries
- 2 tablespoons confectioners' (icing) sugar
- 2 tablespoons water
- 1 cup (250 g) low-fat or fat-free vanilla yogurt

Serves 6 • Preparation 15 minutes + 12 hours to chill • Cooking 15 minutes • Difficulty 2

1. Preheat the oven to 300°F (150°C/gas 2). Oil a six-cup muffin pan with vegetable oil.
2. Beat the egg whites in a large bowl with an electric mixer on medium speed until soft peaks form. Gradually beat in the sugar and vanilla, until stiff, glossy peaks form.
3. Spoon the meringue into the muffin cups. Cover with a sheet of aluminum foil, leaving room for the egg whites to expand. Bake for 15 minutes, until slightly risen and dry, but still spongy. Let cool a little then carefully remove.
4. Mash 1 cup (150 g) of raspberries with the confectioners' sugar in a small bowl until smooth. Stir in the water, then press through a fine-mesh sieve to remove the seeds.
5. Spoon the yogurt into six serving bowls or glasses. Place a soft meringue in each one, and sprinkle with the remaining raspberries. Drizzle with the raspberry sauce and serve.

If you liked this recipe, you will love these as well.

RHUBARB POTS with meringue topping

BANANA mousse

CITRUS & YOGURT syllabub

RICOTTA & BERRY dessert tortillas

- 4 (6-inch/15-cm) flour tortillas
- 8 tablespoons (100 g) seedless raspberry preserves (jam)
- 8 ounces (250 g) low fat ricotta cheese
- 1 cup (150 g) raspberries
- 1 cup (150 g) strawberries, hulled and sliced
- 1 cup (150 g) blueberries

Serves 4 • Preparation 15 minutes • Cooking 5–10 minutes • Difficulty 1

1. Preheat the oven to 350°F (180°C/gas 4). Place the tortillas on a large baking sheet and spread each one with 1 tablespoon of raspberry preserves. Bake until the tortillas are crisp, 5–10 minutes. Let cool to room temperature.
2. Spoon a quarter of the ricotta over each tortilla, spreading it almost to the edge. Divide the berries evenly among the tortillas. Brush the berries with the remaining raspberry preserves, and serve.

BERRY LOW-FAT tiramisù

- 1 cup (200 g) superfine (caster) sugar
- 1 cup (250 ml) water
- 1 cup (150 g) blueberries
- 1 cup (150 g) raspberries
- 8 ounces (250 g) low-fat ricotta cheese
- $^{2}/_{3}$ cup (150 g) light (single) cream cheese
- 1 teaspoon vanilla extract (essence)
- $1^{1}/_{2}$ cups (375 ml) strong black coffee
- $^{1}/_{4}$ cup (60 ml) dry Marsala or sherry
- 8 ladyfingers (sponge fingers), broken into 3 pieces
- 1 tablespoon finely grated dark chocolate

Serves 4 • Preparation 25 minutes + 4 hours to chill • Cooking 7–8 minutes • Difficulty 1

1. Place $^{2}/_{3}$ cup (130 g) of sugar in a saucepan with the water and stir over low heat until the sugar dissolves. Increase the heat to medium and simmer for 5 minutes. Add the blueberries and raspberries and simmer for 2 minutes. Remove from the heat and let cool.
2. Chop the ricotta, cream cheese, vanilla, and remaining $^{1}/_{3}$ cup (70 g) sugar in a food processor until smooth.
3. Mix the coffee and Marsala in a bowl. Dip half the ladyfingers briefly in the coffee mixture. Divide among four serving glasses. Spoon 2 tablespoons of cheese mixture over the top and add some of the berry mixture. Repeat until all the ingredients have been used. Sprinkle with the chocolate. Chill for 4 hours before serving.

FAST fruit parfait

Serves 4–6 • Preparation 10 minutes • Difficulty 1

- 2 cups (500 ml) low-fat or fat-free vanilla yogurt
- 1 cup (150 g) raspberries
- 1 small, sweet fresh pineapple (about 1 pound/500 g), peeled, cored, and cut into small chunks

1. Spoon the yogurt into four to six dessert glasses.
2. Top each glass with the raspberries and pineapple and serve.

LEMON cream

Serves 6 • Preparation 30 minutes + 12 hours to chill
Cooking 10 minutes • Difficulty 1

- 2 cups (500 ml) light (single) cream
- 1/2 cup (100 g) sugar
- 1/3 cup (90 ml) freshly squeezed lemon juice
- 2 tablespoons water
- 2 teaspoons unflavored gelatin
- 1 blood orange, peeled and segmented
- 1 orange, peeled and segmented
- 1 lime, peeled and segmented

1. Stir the cream and sugar in a small saucepan over low heat until the sugar has dissolved. Increase the heat to medium and boil the mixture for 5 minutes. Remove from the heat.
2. Put the lemon juice and water in a small saucepan. Sprinkle with the gelatin and set aside for 5 minutes. Warm over low heat, stirring until the gelatin is dissolved. Let cool a little then stir into the cream. Strain through a fine-mesh sieve into a small bowl. Pour into six dessert glasses and chill overnight.
3. Top each serving of lemon cream with a decorative pile of citrus fruit and serve.

CITRUS & YOGURT syllabub

Serves 6–8 • Preparation 15 minutes + 1 hour to chill
Difficulty 1

- 1/4 cup (60 ml) sweet dessert wine
- 1/4 cup (30 g) confectioners' (icing) sugar
- 1/4 cup (60 ml) freshly squeezed lemon juice
- 2 teaspoons finely grated unwaxed lemon zest
- 2 cups (500 ml) low-fat Greek-style yogurt
- 4 oranges, peeled and segmented

1. Combine the wine, confectioners' sugar, and lemon juice and zest in a small bowl, stirring until the sugar has dissolved.
2. Put the yogurt in a medium bowl and gradually whisk in the wine and lemon mixture.
3. Spoon half of the lemon cream into six to eight serving glasses and cover with half of the orange segments. Repeat with the remaining cream and orange segments.
4. Cover and chill in the refrigerator for at least 1 hour before serving.

SUMMER puddings

Serves 4 • Preparation 30 minutes + 12 hours to chill
Cooking 10 minutes • Difficulty 3

- 18 slices white sandwich bread, crusts removed
- 3 cups (450 g) mixed berries (strawberries, blueberries, raspberries, redcurrants)
- 1/2 cup (100 g) sugar
- 1/2 cup (120 ml) water
- 3/4 cup (180 ml) low-fat or fat-free plain or vanilla yogurt, to serve

1. Line four 1-cup (250-ml) pudding molds with plastic wrap (cling film), allowing extra to hang over the sides. Cut four rounds of bread to fit the bases of the molds and another four slightly larger rounds to fit the tops. Slice the remaining bread into 3/4-inch (2-cm) strips.
2. Put the berries, sugar, and water in a small saucepan over medium heat. Simmer until the berries are tender and releasing their juices, 5–10 minutes. Dip the four smaller bread disks into the berry syrup and put in the molds. Dip the bread strips and line the sides of the molds. Fill with the berry mixture. Place the remaining larger bread disks on top and spoon the syrup over the top. Cover and chill overnight.
3. To serve, invert the puddings onto serving plates. Remove the plastic wrap. Serve with the yogurt passed separately.

Avocados are an excellent source of mono-unsaturated fatty acids, as well as many B vitamins, vitamin E, potassium, and dietary fiber. They are believed to help lower bad cholesterol and to increase good cholesterol.

CHOCOLATE AVOCADO puddings

- 3 avocados, peeled and pitted
- $\frac{1}{2}$ cup (75 g) unsweetened cocoa powder
- $\frac{1}{3}$ cup (90 ml) clear honey
- 1 teaspoon vanilla extract (essence)
- Coarse sea salt, to serve

Serves 4 • Preparation 10 minutes • Difficulty 1

1. Chop the avocados, cocoa, honey, and vanilla in a food processor until smooth.
2. Divide the chocolate avocado mixture evenly among four dessert glasses or bowls. Sprinkle lightly with sea salt and serve at once.

If you liked this recipe, you will love these as well.

LOW-FAT chocolate mousse

LOW-FAT chocolate pudding

LOW-FAT chocolate rice pudding

LOW-FAT chocolate rice pudding

Pudding

- 2 tablespoons unsweetened cocoa powder
- 1/2 cup (100 g) sugar
- Pinch of coarse sea salt
- 5 cups (1.25 liters) skimmed milk
- 1 tablespoon unsalted butter
- 1 cup (200 g) Arborio rice or other short-grain white rice
- 1/4 cup (60 ml) Frangelico
- 2 ounces (60 g) dark chocolate, chopped
- 1/3 cup (90 ml) plain fat-free, Greek-style yogurt

Topping

- 1/2 cup (60 g) blanched hazelnuts, coarsely chopped
- 1 tablespoon lightly beaten egg white
- 4 teaspoons sugar

Serves 6 • Preparation 15 minutes + 2 hours to chill • Cooking 45 minutes • Difficulty 2

Pudding

1. Whisk the cocoa, sugar, salt, and milk in a saucepan over medium heat. Bring to a boil, then remove from the heat.
2. Melt the butter in a medium saucepan over medium heat. Add the rice and cook, stirring constantly, for 2 minutes. Add the milk mixture, bring to a boil, then simmer gently, stirring often, until the rice is tender, about 30 minutes.
3. Remove from the heat. Add the Frangelico and chocolate; stirring until the chocolate has melted. Pour into a bowl. Chill until cold, about 2 hours. Stir in the yogurt.

Topping

1. Preheat the oven to 300°F (150°C/gas 2). Toss the nuts, egg white, and sugar in a bowl. Spread on a baking sheet. Bake for about 15 minutes, stirring often, until the nuts are crisp and golden. Let cool completely on a wire rack.
2. Divide the pudding among serving bowls. Sprinkle with the topping and serve.

LOW-FAT rice pudding

- 3/4 cup (150 g) Arborio rice or other short-grain white rice
- 1/4 cup (50 g) sugar
- 3 cups (750 ml) semi-skimmed milk
- 1 teaspoon vanilla extract (essence)
- Pinch of grated nutmeg
- 1 strip unwaxed lemon zest
- Fresh berries, to serve

Serves 4 • Preparation 15 minutes • Cooking 2 hours • Difficulty 1

1. Preheat the oven to 300°F (150°C/gas 2). Butter a 4-cup (1-liter) baking dish.
2. Add the rice and sugar and stir in the milk and vanilla. Dust with the nutmeg and top with the lemon zest. Bake for 2 hours, until the rice is very tender and the milk is all absorbed.
3. Serve the pudding in small dessert bowls, garnished with the fresh berries.

You will enjoy these delicious little desserts just as much as their full-fat cousins.

LOW-FAT crème caramel

- 1 cup (200 g) sugar
- 2 tablespoons cold water
- 2 large eggs + 2 large egg whites
- 3 cups (750 ml) skimmed milk
- 1 teaspoon vanilla extract (essence)

Serves 8 • Preparation 20 minutes + 4 hours to chill • Cooking 40–50 minutes • Difficulty 1

1. Preheat the oven to 350°F (180°C/gas 4). Set out eight 3/4-cup (180-ml) ramekins.
2. Heat 2/3 cup (130 g) of sugar with the water in a medium saucepan over medium heat until melted and pale gold in color, swirling the pan occasionally. Pour the caramel into the ramekins.
3. Whisk the eggs, egg whites, and remaining 1/3 cup (70 g) of sugar until well blended. Whisk in the milk and vanilla. Pour the custard mixture into the ramekins over the caramel. Set the ramekins in a baking pan. Pour enough boiling water around the ramekins to come halfway up the sides.
4. Bake for 40–50 minutes, until just set. Let cool, then cover, and chill for at least 4 hours.
5. To serve, invert each crème caramel onto a dessert plate, tapping the bottom to help release the custard. Spoon the caramel over the top and serve.

If you liked this recipe, you will love these as well.

47
LOW-FAT panna cotta with passionfruit

80
LOW-FAT crème brûlée

81
LOW-FAT vanilla custards

LOW-FAT crème brûlée

- 1 vanilla pod
- 1 1/4 cups (300 ml) light (single) cream
- 1/4 cup (60 ml) skimmed milk
- 3 large egg yolks
- 1/4 cup (50 g) superfine (caster) sugar
- 1/2 cup (100 g) firmly packed light brown sugar

Serves 4 • Preparation 20 minutes + 5 hours to infuse & chill • Cooking 40–50 minutes • Difficulty 1

1. Preheat the oven to 300°F (150°C/gas 2). Oil four 3/4-cup (180-ml) ramekins. Spilt the vanilla pod in half lengthwise and use a knife to scrape out the seeds. Combine the seeds in a saucepan with the cream and milk. Place over medium heat and bring to a boil. Remove from the heat and set aside for 1 hour to allow the flavors to infuse.
2. Beat the egg yolks and sugar in a bowl with an electric mixer on high speed until pale and creamy. Beat in the cream and milk. Strain through a fine-mesh sieve. Pour into the ramekins. Set the ramekins in a baking pan. Pour enough boiling water around the ramekins to come halfway up the sides.
3. Bake for 35–45 minutes, until set but still wobbly in the center. Let cool, then chill for at least 4 hours.
4. Sprinkle some brown sugar over each ramekin. Preheat the broiler (grill) on high. Broil until the sugar turns a golden color, 3–5 minutes. Serve immediately.

LOW-FAT vanilla custards

- 2 cups (500 ml) skimmed milk
- 1/2 cup (100 g) superfine (caster) sugar
- 1 teaspoon vanilla extract (essence)
- 2 large eggs

Serves 4 • Preparation 15 minutes + 4 hours to chill • Cooking 15–20 minutes • Difficulty 1

1. Preheat the oven to 325°F (170°C/gas 3). Oil four 3/4-cup (180-ml) ramekins.
2. Combine the milk in a small saucepan with the sugar and vanilla. Bring to a gentle boil, stirring to dissolve the sugar. Remove from the heat and cool for a few minutes.
3. Whisk the eggs in a small bowl until frothy. Slowly whisk into the milk.
4. Set the ramekins in a roasting pan and divide the custard evenly among them. Pour enough boiling water around the ramekins to come halfway up the sides.
5. Bake for 15–20 minutes, until just set. Let cool and then chill for at least 4 hours before serving.

cakes & bakes

GLUTEN-FREE chocolate layer cake

Serves 12 • Preparation 45 minutes • Cooking 1 hour • Difficulty 3

Cake
- 1½ cups (300 g) sugar
- ¾ cup (120 g) brown rice flour
- ½ cup (75 g) finely ground almonds
- ¾ cup (120 g) unsweetened cocoa powder
- ¼ cup (30 g) quinoa flour
- 2 teaspoons baking soda (bicarbonate of soda)
- 1 teaspoon baking powder
- ½ teaspoon salt
- 2 large eggs, lightly beaten
- ¾ cup (180 ml) warm water
- ¾ cup (180 ml) skimmed milk
- 2 tablespoons unsalted butter
- 1 teaspoon vanilla extract (essence)

Seven-Minute Frosting
- 1¼ cups (250 g) sugar
- ¼ cup (60 ml) water
- 1 tablespoon + 1 teaspoon corn (golden) syrup
- 5 large egg whites
- ¾ teaspoon vanilla extract (essence)
- Pink food coloring
- ⅛ teaspoon salt
- Fresh raspberries, to decorate

Cake

1. Preheat the oven to 350°F (180°C/gas 4). Oil two 8-inch (20-cm) cake pans. Line with parchment paper.
2. Combine the sugar, brown rice flour, almonds, cocoa, quinoa flour, baking soda, baking powder, and salt in a large bowl. Add the eggs, water, milk, butter, and vanilla and beat until smooth and well mixed. Divide the batter evenly between the prepared pans.
3. Bake for 1 hour, until the cakes pull away from the sides of the pans. Let cool in the pans on a wire rack for 10 minutes. Turn out of the pans onto the rack, carefully remove the paper, and let cool completely.

Seven-Minute Frosting

1. Combine the sugar, water, corn syrup, and egg whites in a double boiler over barely simmering water. Cook, whisking occasionally, until the sugar dissolves and the mixture registers 160°F (80°C) on a candy thermometer.
2. Beat the hot sugar mixture with a mixer on high speed until stiff, glossy peaks form, about 7 minutes. Beat in the vanilla, food coloring, and salt.
3. Place one cake layer on a plate. Spread with two cups of frosting. Place the remaining cake layer on top. Frost the top and sides of the cake with the remaining frosting. Decorate with the raspberries and serve.

Low-fat or skimmed ricotta cheese has about a third less fat than regular ricotta cheese, without losing any of its sweet and creamy flavor. However, you should bear in mind that like all cheese, even low-fat ricotta is quite high in fat. Ricotta is a very good source of protein and also a good source of calcium, phosphorus, and selenium.

LOW-FAT ricotta cheesecake

Cheesecake

- 1/2 cup (100 g) sugar
- 2 pounds (1 kg) low-fat fresh ricotta cheese, drained
- 1/2 cup (120 ml) lemon curd
- 1 teaspoon vanilla extract (essence)
- 1 tablespoon finely grated zest of 1 unwaxed lemon
- 1/3 cup (50 g) cornstarch (cornflour)
- 4 large eggs, lightly beaten

Apricot Topping

- 1 cup (200 g) sugar
- 1 1/4 cups (300 ml) cold water
- 8 ounces (250 g) dried apricots
- 2 tablespoons sweet white wine
- 1/2 teaspoon saffron threads
- 1 cinnamon stick
- 6 cardamom pods, bruised
- Confectioners' (icing) sugar, to dust

Serves 8-12 • Preparation 45 minutes + 2-3 hours to chill • Cooking 1 hour • Difficulty 2

Cheesecake

1. Preheat the oven to 325°F (170°C/gas 3). Oil an 8-inch (20-cm) springform pan.
2. Combine the sugar, ricotta, lemon curd, vanilla, lemon zest, and cornstarch in a food processor and pulse to combine. Add the eggs and process until smooth. Pour into the prepared pan, smoothing the top.
3. Bake for 40–45 minutes, until a toothpick inserted into the center comes out clean. Turn off the oven, leave the door slightly ajar, and let the cheesecake cool completely.
4. Chill the cheesecake for 2–3 hours.

Apricot Topping

1. Combine the sugar and water in a medium saucepan over low heat and stir until the sugar dissolves. Add the apricots, wine, saffron, cinnamon, and cardamom. Simmer over low heat until the apricots are tender and the sauce has reduced, 15–20 minutes. Set aside and let cool completely.
2. Dust the cheesecake with confectioners' sugar, spoon the apricot mixture over the top, and serve.

GLUTEN-FREE almond torte with pears

Torte

- $1^1/_4$ cups (180 g) whole almonds, toasted
- 1 teaspoon cornstarch (cornflour)
- 4 large eggs, separated
- $^3/_4$ cup (150 g) sugar
- 2 teaspoons finely grated unwaxed lemon zest
- $^1/_2$ teaspoon vanilla extract (essence)
- $^1/_2$ teaspoon salt

Pears

- 4 cups (1 liter) water
- $^3/_4$ cup (150 g) sugar + 2 tablespoons extra
- 1 cinnamon stick
- Strips of zest from 1 unwaxed lemon
- 4 firm, ripe pears, peeled, cored, and quartered
- 1 cup (250 ml) low-fat or fat-free vanilla yogurt, to serve

Serves 8 • Preparation 45 minutes • Cooking 40–50 minutes
Difficulty 2

Torte

1. Preheat the oven to 350°F (180°C/gas 4). Oil a 9-inch (23-cm) springform pan. Chop the almonds and cornstarch in a food processor until finely ground.
2. Beat the egg yolks, sugar, lemon zest, vanilla, and salt until pale and thick. Fold in the almond mixture. Whisk the egg whites until stiff peaks form. Fold into the almond mixture until just combined. Pour the batter into the prepared pan.
3. Bake for 25–30 minutes, until a toothpick inserted into the center comes out clean. Let cool in the pan.

Pears

1. Bring the water, sugar, cinnamon, and lemon zest to a boil. Add the pears and simmer over low heat until tender when pierced with a paring knife, about 15 minutes. Transfer to a plate with a slotted spoon. Bring the liquid to a boil and simmer until thick and syrupy, 15–20 minutes. Let cool.
2. Serve the torte with the pears, syrup, and yogurt.

LOW-FAT carrot cake

Serves 8-10 • Preparation 30 minutes • Cooking 1 hour • Difficulty 1

Cake

- 1 1/3 cups (150 g) shredded carrots
- 3 cups (750 ml) water
- 2 cups (300 g) all-purpose (plain) flour
- 2 cups (400 g) sugar
- 2 teaspoons baking soda (bicarbonate of soda)
- 2 teaspoons ground cinnamon
- 1/2 cup (120 ml) light, mild-flavored extra-virgin olive oil
- 1/2 cup (120 ml) applesauce
- 5 large egg whites
- 2 teaspoons vanilla extract (essence)
- 1/4 cup (30 g) chopped walnuts
- 1/2 cup (75 g) shredded (desiccated) coconut
- 1/2 cup (100 g) canned crushed pineapple, drained

Frosting

- 4 ounces (120 g) fat-free cream cheese, softened
- 3/4 cup (120 g) confectioners' (icing) sugar
- 3/4 teaspoon vanilla extract (essence)
- 1 teaspoon freshly squeezed lemon juice

Cake

1. Preheat the oven to 350°F (180°C/gas 4). Oil a 9 x 13-inch (23 x 33-cm) cake pan. Dust with flour.
2. Put the carrots and water in a saucepan. Bring to a boil and simmer for 5 minutes. Drain and set aside to cool. Combine the flour, sugar, baking soda, and cinnamon in a large bowl.
3. Beat the oil, applesauce, egg whites, and vanilla in a large bowl. Add the flour mixture and beat until well blended. Fold in the carrots, walnuts, coconut, and pineapple.
4. Spoon the batter into the prepared pan. Bake for 1 hour, until firm and golden. Let cool in the pan on a wire rack for 10 minutes. Turn out onto the rack and let cool completely.

Frosting

1. Beat the cream cheese in a small bowl. Stir in the confectioners' sugar, vanilla, and lemon juice. Frost the cake and serve.

Serve this hearty cake for brunch at the weekend. It is filled with energy and goodness and will keep you going throughout the day.

DATE & WALNUT CAKE with sauce

Cake

- 3/4 cup (120 g) old-fashioned (quick-cooking) rolled oats
- 1 cup (250 ml) boiling water
- 1/4 cup (50 g) firmly packed light brown sugar
- 1/4 cup (60 ml) clear honey
- 1/4 cup (60 ml) light, mild-flavored extra-virgin olive oil
- 2 large eggs
- 1 teaspoon vanilla extract (essence)
- 3/4 cup (120 g) all-purpose (plain) flour
- 1/2 cup (75 g) whole-wheat (wholemeal) flour
- 1 teaspoon ground cinnamon
- 1/2 teaspoon baking soda (bicarbonate of soda)
- 1/4 teaspoon ground nutmeg
- 1/8 teaspoon salt
- 1/3 cup (90 ml) skimmed milk
- 1/4 cup (30 g) chopped dates
- 2 tablespoons chopped walnuts

Sauce

- 1/2 cup (120 ml) skimmed milk
- 1/4 teaspoon ground nutmeg
- 1/4 cup (60 ml) clear honey

Serves 8 • Preparation 45 minutes • Cooking 35–40 minutes
Difficulty 2

Cake

1. Preheat the oven to 350°F (180°C/gas 4). Oil a 9-inch (23-cm) round cake pan.
2. Combine the oats and boiling water in a bowl. Let stand until the water is absorbed, about 20 minutes. Stir in the brown sugar, honey, and oil. Add the eggs, one at a time, beating well after each addition. Stir in the vanilla.
3. Combine both flours, the cinnamon, baking soda, nutmeg and salt in a bowl. Add the flour mixture to the oat mixture, then stir in the milk. Stir in the dates and walnuts.
4. Spoon the batter into the prepared pan and bake for 25–30 minutes, until a toothpick inserted into the center comes out clean. Place the pan on a wire rack to cool slightly.

Sauce

1. Combine the milk and nutmeg in a small saucepan over medium heat and bring to a simmer. Stir in the honey, increase the heat to medium, and bring to a boil, stirring constantly. Simmer until the mixture thickens slightly, about 3 minutes.
2. Cut the cake into eight wedges and serve warm with the sauce spooned over the top.

GLUTEN-FREE chocolate roulade

Roulade

4	large eggs
3/4	cup (150 g) superfine (caster) sugar
1/2	teaspoon vanilla extract (essence)
1/3	cup (50 g) unsweetened cocoa powder
2	tablespoons rice flour
1/4	cup (60 g) salted butter, melted
	Confectioners' (icing) sugar, for dusting
2	tablespoons coarsely grated dark chocolate

Filling

8	ounces (250 g) low-fat cream cheese, softened
2/3	cup (100 g) confectioners' (icing) sugar
2	tablespoons freshly squeezed lemon juice
1/4	cup (60 g) lemon curd

Serves 6–8 • Preparation 30 minutes + 30 minutes to chill • Cooking 20 minutes • Difficulty 3

Roulade

1. Preheat the oven to 350°F (180°C/gas 4). Line a 9 x 13-inch (23 x 33-cm) jelly-roll pan with parchment paper.
2. Beat the eggs, sugar, and vanilla in a bowl with an electric mixer on medium speed until pale and thick. Sift the cocoa and rice flour and fold into the egg mixture. Gently fold in the melted butter. Spoon the batter into the pan.
3. Bake for 20 minutes, until springy when pressed in the center. Leave in the pan for 5 minutes to cool. Dust a clean kitchen towel with confectioners' sugar. Turn the cake out onto the towel. Roll up the cake, using the towel as a guide. Leave, seam-side down, until cool.

Filling

1. Beat the cream cheese until smooth. Beat in the confectioners' sugar, lemon juice, and lemon curd. Spread over the cake and roll up. Sprinkle with the confectioners' sugar and chocolate. Chill for 30 minutes before serving.

GLUTEN-FREE chocolate cake

Cake

- 3 tablespoons salted butter
- 6 ounces (180 g) dark chocolate, chopped
- 6 large eggs, separated
- 1 cup (200 g) sugar
- 3 tablespoons instant coffee powder
- 1 tablespoon vanilla extract (essence)

Mocha Glaze

- 3 ounces (90 g) dark chocolate, chopped
- 2 tablespoons salted butter
- 2 teaspoons vanilla extract (essence)
- 1/3 cup (90 ml) light (single) cream
- 1/3 cup (70 g) sugar
- 1 tablespoon instant espresso powder

Serves 8 • Preparation 15 minutes • Cooking 40–45 minutes
Difficulty 2

Cake

1. Preheat the oven to 350°F (180°C/gas 4). Butter a 9-inch (23-cm) springform pan. Melt the butter and chocolate in a double boiler over barely simmering water.
2. Beat the egg yolks with half the sugar until pale and thick. Beat in the coffee, vanilla, and chocolate mixture. Beat the egg whites until foamy. Beat in the remaining sugar, until stiff peaks form. Fold into the chocolate mixture. Spoon into the prepared pan.
3. Bake for 40–45 minutes, until set. Let cool completely in the pan on a wire rack. Remove the pan sides when cool.

Mocha Glaze

1. Put the chocolate, butter, and vanilla in a bowl. Bring the cream, sugar, and coffee to a boil. Pour over the chocolate, stirring until smooth. Drizzle over the cake and serve warm.

Angel food cakes are light, airy foam cakes made without egg yolk or fat. They are not hard to make if you follow a few simple rules. Make sure the egg whites are at warm room temperature and do not overbeat them. Beat slowly at first to develop plenty of air cells, then beat faster as the foam develops. Beat in the sugar until the whites are almost stiff, then gently fold in the dry ingredients. Do not stir the batter, or the fragile air cells will deflate. Gently pour and spoon the batter into the prepared pan as soon as it is ready; don't let it sit around before baking. Make sure the oven is heated to the right temperature ahead of time.

ANGEL FOOD CAKE with compote

Cake

- 12 large egg whites, at room temperature
- 1 teaspoon cream of tartar
- $1\frac{1}{2}$ cups (300 g) superfine (caster) sugar
- 1 tablespoon finely grated unwaxed orange zest
- 1 cup (150 g) cake flour

Compote

- $1\frac{1}{3}$ cups (320 ml) water
- 14 ounces (400 g) dried apricots, halved
- 1 cup (100 g) dried cranberries
- $\frac{2}{3}$ cup (150 ml) freshly squeezed orange juice
- $\frac{1}{3}$ cup (70 g) sugar
- 1 (2-inch/5-cm) stick cinnamon
- $\frac{1}{2}$ teaspoon vanilla extract (essence)
- $\frac{1}{4}$ teaspoon almond extract (essence)

Serves 8–12 • Preparation 25 minutes • Cooking 40 minutes
Difficulty 2

Cake

1. Preheat the oven to 350°F (180°C/gas 4). Set out a 10-inch (25-cm) angel food pan. Beat the egg whites and cream of tartar with an electric mixer on medium speed until soft peaks form. Gradually add the sugar, beating until stiff peaks form. Sprinkle with the orange zest. Sift in the flour. Fold in gently. Spoon the batter into the prepared pan.
2. Bake for 40 minutes, until springy to the touch. Invert the cake on the legs of the pan, or over a bottle if your pan doesn't have legs. Let cool. Unmold and slice to serve.

Compote

1. Combine the water, apricots, cranberries, orange juice, sugar, cinnamon, vanilla, and almond extract in a saucepan and bring to a boil. Cover and simmer for 10 minutes. Remove from the heat and discard the cinnamon. Spoon over the slices of cake and serve.

If you liked this recipe, you will love these as well.

86
GLUTEN-FREE almond torte with pears

87
LOW-FAT carrot cake

95
RASPBERRY & ALMOND cake

GLUTEN-FREE dried fruit balls

- 2 cups (500 ml) skimmed milk
- 1/4 cup (50 g) firmly packed dark brown sugar
- 2 tablespoons clear honey
- 1/4 teaspoon ground cardamom
- 1/4 teaspoon salt
- 1/2 cup (100 g) Arborio rice
- 1/2 cup (60 g) golden raisins (sultanas)
- 1/2 cup (75 g) unsweetened shredded (desiccated) coconut
- 1/2 cup (60 g) whole almonds

Makes 20–24 • Preparation 20 minutes + 3 hours to chill • Cooking 30–35 minutes • Difficulty 2

1. Combine the milk, brown sugar, honey, cardamom, and salt in a medium saucepan and bring to a boil. Add the rice, partially cover, and simmer, stirring occasionally, until very tender, 30–35 minutes.
2. Transfer the rice to a bowl and stir in the golden raisins. Cover and chill until cold, at least 2 hours.
3. Preheat the oven to 375°F (190°/gas 5). Spread the coconut and almonds on a rimmed baking sheet and bake for 5–7 minutes, until golden. Grind in a food processor until coarsely ground. Set aside.
4. Form tablespoons of the rice mixture into balls and roll in the nut and coconut mixture. Chill until firm, at least 1 hour.

RASPBERRY & ALMOND cake

- 1 cup (150 g) all-purpose flour
- $^1/_3$ cup (70 g) sugar
- 5 tablespoons (75 g) salted butter, chilled
- $^1/_2$ cup (120 ml) low-fat vanilla yogurt
- $1^1/_4$ teaspoons vanilla extract (essence)
- $^1/_2$ teaspoon almond extract (essence)
- 1 large egg
- $^1/_2$ teaspoon baking powder
- $^1/_4$ teaspoon baking soda (bicarbonate of soda)
- 4 ounces (120 g) low-fat cream cheese, softened
- $^1/_3$ cup (100 g) seedless raspberry preserves (jam)
- 1 cup (150 g) fresh raspberries
- 3 tablespoons chopped almonds

Serves 8 • Preparation 15 minutes + 3 hours to chill • Cooking 40–45 minutes • Difficulty 1

1. Preheat the oven to 350°F (180°C/gas 4). Oil an 8-inch (20-cm) baking pan. Combine the flour and sugar in a large bowl. Rub in the butter with your fingers until crumbly. Reserve ½ cup of the mixture for later use.
2. Add the yogurt, vanilla, almond, egg, baking powder, and baking soda to the remaining mixture. Beat until blended. Pour into the pan.
3. Combine the cream cheese and raspberry preserves in a small bowl and beat until blended. Spread over batter. Top with the reserved flour mixture, raspberries, and almonds.
4. Bake for 40–45 minutes, until browned. Cool on a rack. Chill for 3 hours before serving.

SUGAR-FREE berry cupcakes

Makes 12 • Preparation 25 minutes • Cooking 25–30 minutes • Difficulty 1

- 1 1/4 cups (180 g) all-purpose (plain) flour
- 2 tablespoons finely ground almonds
- 1 teaspoon baking powder
- 1/8 teaspoon salt
- 1/2 cup (120 g) unsalted butter, softened
- 1/3 cup (90 ml) clear honey
- 1 teaspoon finely grated unwaxed lemon zest
- 2 large eggs
- 1/4 cup (60 ml) milk
- 1 cup (150 g) blueberries, mashed

1. Preheat the oven to 325°F (170°C/gas 3). Line a standard 12-cup muffin tin with paper liners. Combine the flour, almonds, baking powder, and salt in a small bowl.
2. Beat the butter, honey, and lemon zest in a bowl with an electric mixer on medium speed until pale and creamy. Add the eggs one at a time, beating until just blended after each addition. With the mixer on low speed, add the flour mixture and milk. Stir the blueberries in by hand.
3. Spoon the batter into the prepared cups. Bake for 25–30 minutes, until golden brown. Transfer the muffin tin to a wire rack and let cool.

DAIRY-FREE cupcakes

Makes 12 • Preparation 40 minutes • Cooking 20–25 minutes • Difficulty 2

- 1 cup (150 g) all-purpose (plain) flour
- 2 teaspoons baking powder
- 1/2 cup (125 g) dairy-free spread
- 1/2 cup (100 g) sugar
- 1 teaspoon rosewater
- 2 large eggs, beaten
- 1/4 cup (60 ml) soy milk
- 12 squares Turkish delight
- 1 1/2 cups (225 g) confectioners' (icing) sugar
- 2 tablespoons water
- Red food coloring

1. Preheat the oven to 350°F (180°C/gas 4). Line a standard 12-cup muffin tin with paper liners. Combine the flour and baking powder in a bowl.
2. Beat the dairy-free spread, sugar, and rosewater until creamy. Add the eggs. With the mixer on low speed, add the flour mixture and soy milk. Spoon the batter into the prepared cups. Press a square of Turkish delight into each one. Bake for 20–25 minutes, until golden brown. Transfer the muffin tin to a wire rack.
3. Mix the confectioners' sugar and water in a bowl. Put a quarter of the mixture in a small bowl and tint red with the food coloring. Spread the white frosting over the cupcakes. Use the red frosting to decorate.

EGG-FREE cupcakes

Makes 12 • Preparation 15 minutes • Cooking 25–30 minutes • Difficulty 1

- 6 ounces (180 g) dark chocolate, chopped
- 1/3 cup (90 g) salted butter
- 1 1/2 cups (225 g) all-purpose (plain) flour
- 3/4 cup (150 g) sugar
- 2 tablespoons unsweetened cocoa powder
- 1 1/2 teaspoons baking powder
- 1 teaspoon baking soda
- 1 cup (250 ml) milk
- 1 cup (150 g) mixed berries + extra, to decorate
- 1/4 cup (60 ml) light (single) cream

1. Preheat the oven to 325°F (170°C/gas 3). Line a standard 12-cup muffin tin with paper liners. Melt the chocolate and butter in a double boiler over barely simmering water.
2. Combine the flour, sugar, cocoa, baking powder, and baking soda in a bowl. Pour half the melted chocolate and milk into the flour mixture and mix until just combined. Stir the berries in by hand. Spoon the batter into the prepared cups.
3. Bake for 25–30 minutes, until risen and firm to the touch. Transfer to a wire rack. Let cool completely before removing the cupcakes.
4. Stir the cream into the remaining chocolate mixture. Spread over the cupcakes and top with extra berries.

DIABETIC cupcakes

Makes 16 • Preparation 20 minutes + 15 minutes to rest Cooking 25–30 minutes • Difficulty 2

- 2 (14-ounce/400-g) can pears, in natural syrup
- 1 cup (100 g) old-fashioned (quick-cooking) rolled oats
- 1 cup (150 g) all-purpose (plain) flour
- 1 cup (150 g) whole-wheat (wholemeal) flour
- 1 teaspoon baking soda
- 1/2 teaspoon baking powder
- 2 teaspoons ground ginger
- 1/2 cup (125 g) low-fat dairy-free spread
- 3/4 cup (150 g) brown sugar
- 1 teaspoon vanilla extract
- 2 large eggs, beaten
- 2 tablespoons flaked almonds

1. Preheat the oven to 325°F (170°C/gas 3). Line two 12-cup muffin tins with 16 paper liners. Drain the pear syrup into a small saucepan. Add the oats and bring to a boil. Set aside for 15 minutes.
2. Thinly slice two pear halves for decoration. The other pears can be served separately. Combine both flours, the baking soda, baking powder, and ginger in a bowl. Beat the dairy-free spread, brown sugar, and vanilla until creamy. Add the eggs. Beat in the flour and oat mixtures. Spoon into the cups. Top with the sliced pears and almonds.
3. Bake for 25–30 minutes, until golden brown and firm to the touch. Transfer to a wire rack and let cool.

LOW-FAT chocolate soufflés

- 1/2 cup (75 g) unsweetened cocoa powder
- 6 tablespoons hot water
- 1 tablespoon unsalted butter
- 1 tablespoon canola oil
- 3 tablespoons all-purpose (plain) flour
- 1 tablespoon ground hazelnuts
- 1/4 teaspoon ground cinnamon
- 3 tablespoons firmly packed dark brown sugar
- 2 tablespoons honey
- 1/8 teaspoon salt
- 3/4 cup (180 ml) skimmed milk
- 4 large egg whites
- 3 tablespoons sugar
- 2 teaspoons confectioners' (icing) sugar
- 1 cup (150 g) raspberries, to serve

Serves 6 • Preparation 15 minutes • Cooking 15–20 minutes • Difficulty 3

1. Preheat the oven to 375°F (190°C/gas 5). Oil six 1-cup (250-ml) souffle dishes. Stir the cocoa and hot water in a medium bowl until smooth. Set aside.
2. Melt the butter in a small saucepan over low heat. Add the oil and stir to combine. Add the flour, hazelnuts, and cinnamon and cook for 1 minute, stirring constantly. Stir in the brown sugar, honey, and salt. Gradually add the milk and cook, stirring constantly, until thickened, about 3 minutes. Stir into the cocoa mixture. Let cool slightly.
3. Beat the egg whites until foamy. Add the sugar and beat until stiff peaks form. Fold the egg whites into the cocoa mixture. Gently spoon the batter into the prepared dishes.
4. Bake for 15–20 minutes, until risen and set in the center. Cool on a wire rack for 10 minutes. Dust with the confectioners' sugar and serve warm with the raspberries.

GLUTEN-FREE chocolate cupcakes

- 1/3 cup (90 g) unsalted butter
- 8 ounces (250 g) dark chocolate, coarsely chopped
- 6 large eggs, separated
- 1/2 cup (100 g) sugar
- Vanilla ice cream, to serve
- Fresh raspberries, to serve

Makes 20 • Preparation 20 minutes • Cooking 25–30 minutes
Difficulty 1

1. Preheat the oven to 275°F (140°C/gas 1). Line two 12-cup standard muffin tins with 20 paper liners. Melt the butter and chocolate in a double boiler over barely simmering water. Let cool slightly then whisk in the egg yolks.
2. Beat the egg whites until soft peaks form. Gradually add the sugar, beating until stiff and glossy. Fold into the chocolate mixture. Spoon the batter into the muffin cups.
3. Bake for 20–25 minutes, until firm to the touch. Transfer to wire racks and let cool completely. The centers of the cupcakes will sink. Fill with a scoop of vanilla ice cream, scatter with a few raspberries, and serve.

These pretty cream puffs make a striking dessert and will be a welcome addition to any buffet spread. With their yogurt cream filling and fresh fruit sauce, they are much healthier than traditional cream puffs.

BERRY & YOGURT puffs

Yogurt Cream

2 cups (500 ml) plain Greek-style yogurt
2 tablespoons confectioners' (icing) sugar
1 teaspoon vanilla extract (essence)

Choux Puffs

2 large eggs + 3 large egg whites
1 cup (250 ml) water
3 tablespoons salted butter
1 cup (150 g) all-purpose (plain) flour

Strawberry Sauce

2 cups (300 g) fresh strawberries, hulled
2 tablespoons confectioners' (icing) sugar
1 teaspoon finely grated unwaxed orange zest
1 tablespoon freshly squeezed orange juice

Makes 12 • Preparation 45 minutes + 4 hours to chill • Cooking 25-30 minutes • Difficulty 3

Yogurt Cream

1. Spoon the yogurt into a fine-mesh sieve. Cover, place over a bowl, and chill for 4 hours. Stir in the confectioners' sugar and vanilla.

Choux Puffs

1. Preheat the oven to 425°F (220°C/gas 7). Line a baking sheet with parchment paper. Whisk the eggs and egg whites in a small bowl. Set aside. Stir the water and butter in a saucepan over medium heat and bring to a boil. Remove from the heat, add the flour and quickly mix. Stir over medium heat until the mixture forms a ball, about 1 minute. Remove from the heat. Set aside for 5 minutes. Add the egg mixture, a little at a time, until smooth and glossy.
2. Place 12 heaped dessertspoons of choux mixture onto the prepared baking sheet and sprinkle with water. Reduce the oven temperature to 400°F (200°C/gas 6). Bake for 25-30 minutes, until puffed and lightly browned. Make a cut the the side of each puff and return to oven for 5 minutes. Turn off the oven and leave the puffs inside until cooled.

Berry Sauce

1. Blend the strawberries, confectioners' sugar, orange zest, and juice to a purée. Pour into a bowl.
2. Cut the puffs in half and remove any doughy pastry inside. Fill each puff with yogurt cream. Spoon the strawberry sauce over the top, and serve.

GLUTEN-FREE chocolate peanut cookies

- 1 cup (250 g) smooth peanut butter
- 3/4 cup (150 g) sugar
- 1 large egg, lightly beaten
- 1/2 teaspoon baking soda (bicarbonate of soda)
- 3/4 cup (120 g) dark chocolate chips
- 1/2 cup (60 g) roasted salted peanuts

Makes 16–20 • Preparation 15 minutes • Cooking 12–15 minutes
Difficulty 1

1. Preheat the oven to 350°F (180°C/gas 4). Line two baking sheets with parchment paper.
2. Beat the peanut butter, sugar, egg, and baking soda until well combined. Stir in the chocolate chips and peanuts.
3. With lightly floured hands, roll tablespoons of the dough into balls. Place 2 inches (5 cm) apart on the prepared baking sheets.
4. Bake for 12–15 minutes, until golden brown. Cool for 5 minutes on the baking sheets, then transfer to wire racks and let cool completely.

ORANGE meringues

- 4 large egg whites
- $1\frac{1}{4}$ cups (250 g) superfine (caster) sugar
- 1 teaspoon cornstarch (cornflour)
- 1 teaspoon white wine vinegar
- 1 teaspoon vanilla extract (essence)
- Finely grated zest of 1 unwaxed orange
- $\frac{1}{2}$ teaspoon orange or yellow food coloring

Makes 18–20 • Preparation 25 minutes • Cooking 1 hour • Difficulty 1

1. Preheat the oven to 275°F (140°C/gas 1). Line two baking sheets with baking parchment.
2. Beat the egg whites in a large bowl with an electric mixer on medium speed until soft peaks form. Gradually beat in the sugar, cornstarch, vinegar, vanilla, and orange zest until smooth and glossy. Fold in the food coloring.
3. Spoon the meringue into a piping bag. Pipe 18–20 spirals onto the prepared baking sheets, spacing well.
4. Bake for 1 hour. Decrease the oven temperature to 250°F (130°C/gas $\frac{1}{2}$) after 30 minutes. Cool on the parchment paper on a wire rack.

Irresistible lemon tart is usually off-limits for those following a low-fat diet. Here we have reduced the amount of butter and eggs to make a tart that has less fat than traditional recipes, without sacrificing any of the tart's creamy goodness.

LOWER-FAT lemon tart

Crust

- 1 cup (150 g) all-purpose (plain) flour
- 1 tablespoon confectioners' (icing) sugar
- 1/4 cup (60 g) salted butter, chilled and cut up
- 1 tablespoon vegetable oil
- 1 large egg yolk
- 1–2 tablespoons ice water

Filling

- 1 cup (150 g) confectioners' (icing) sugar + extra, to dust
- 3 large eggs + 2 large egg whites, lightly beaten together
- 2 tablespoons finely grated unwaxed lemon zest
- 1/2 cup (120 ml) freshly squeezed lemon juice
- 3/4 cup (180 ml) half-fat crème fraîche

Serves 12 • Preparation 45 minutes + 15 minutes to chill & 1–2 hours to cool • Cooking 50–60 minutes • Difficulty 2

Crust

1. Combine the flour and confectioners' sugar in a medium bowl. Rub in the butter until the mixture resembles fine bread crumbs. Stir in the oil, egg yolk, and enough ice water to bring the dough together. Shape into a ball.
2. Roll out on a lightly floured work surface to fit a 9-inch (23-cm) pie pan with a removeable bottom. Place in the pan, trimming the edges. Lightly prick with a fork, then chill for 15 minutes. Preheat the oven to 375° (190°C/gas 5).
3. Line the chilled pastry case with parchment paper and baking weights or dried beans and bake for 20 minutes, until well set. Remove the weights and paper, then bake for 5 more minutes, until pale golden brown.

Filling

1. Put the confectioners' sugar in a bowl and gradually whisk in the eggs. Stir in the lemon zest and juice. Set aside.
2. Strain the lemon mixture through a fine-mesh sieve. Beat the crème fraîche in a medium bowl until smooth, then slowly stir into the lemon mixture. Pour into the warm pastry case.
3. Decrease the oven temperature to 300°F (150°C/gas 2). Bake for 25–30 minutes, until the filling is just set, and still a little wobbly in the center.
4. Let cool for 1–2 hours. Dust with a little extra confectioners' sugar and serve.

LOW-FAT chocolate frozen yogurt kisses

- 1/2 cup (75 g) unsweetened cocoa powder
- 1/2 cup (75 g) all-purpose (plain) flour
- 3/4 teaspoon cinnamon
- 1/4 teaspoon salt
- 2 tablespoons unsalted butter, softened
- 1/4 cup (50 g) firmly packed dark brown sugar
- 1/4 cup (50 g) sugar
- 1/2 teaspoon vanilla extract (essence)
- 1 large egg white
- 1 cup (250 ml) fat-free frozen vanilla yogurt

Makes 12–16 • Preparation 15 minutes + 15 minutes to chill • Cooking 10–12 minutes • Difficulty 1

1. Preheat the oven to 350°F (180°C/gas 4). Line two baking sheets with parchment paper.
2. Combine the cocoa, flour, cinnamon, and salt in a bowl. Beat the butter, both sugars, and vanilla with an electric mixer on medium speed until creamy. Add the egg white and beat to combine. With the mixer on low speed, beat in the flour mixture. Shape the dough into a ball, wrap in plastic wrap (cling film), and chill for 15 minutes.
3. Drop heaped teaspoons of dough onto the prepared baking sheets. Flatten slightly with the palm of your hand. Bake for 10–12 minutes, until firm. Cool on a wire rack.
4. Spoon about one tablespoon of frozen yogurt onto half the cookies and sandwich together with the remaining cookies. Serve at once.

LOW-FAT strawberry shortcake

- $1^{3}/_{4}$ cups (270 g) whole-wheat (wholemeal) flour
- $^{1}/_{4}$ cup (30 g) all-purpose (plain) flour
- $2^{1}/_{2}$ teaspoons baking powder
- 1 tablespoon sugar
- $^{1}/_{4}$ cup (60 g) trans-free margarine, chilled
- $^{3}/_{4}$ cup (180 ml) fat-free milk, chilled
- 2 cups (300 g) strawberries, hulled and sliced
- $^{1}/_{4}$ cup (60 ml) fat-free vanilla yogurt

Makes 8 • Preparation 15 minutes • Cooking 10–12 minutes • Difficulty 1

1. Preheat the oven to 350°F (180°C/gas 4). Line a baking sheet with parchment paper.
2. Combine both flours, the baking powder and sugar in a bowl. Cut in the chilled margarine with a fork until the mixture resembles coarse bread crumbs. Add the milk and stir until a moist dough forms.
3. Turn out onto a floured work surface and knead until smooth. Roll into a rectangle about $^{1}/_{4}$ inch (5 mm) thick. Cut into eight squares. Place on the prepared baking sheet. Bake for 10–12 minutes, until golden.
4. Transfer the shortcake to serving plates. Top with the strawberries and yogurt and serve warm.

CHEWY OAT, SEED & FRUIT bars

- 2 cups (300 g) old-fashioned (quick-cooking) rolled oats
- 1/2 cup (75 g) sunflower seeds
- 1/3 cup (50 g) shredded (desiccated) coconut
- 1/3 cup (50 g) all-purpose (plain) flour
- 3/4 cup (180 g) unsalted butter
- 3/4 cup (180 g) corn (golden) syrup
- 3/4 cup (150 g) firmly packed light brown sugar
- 1 cup (120 g) dried apricots, coarsely chopped
- 1/2 cup (120 g) crunchy peanut butter
- 1 teaspoon vanilla extract (essence)

Makes 18–20 • Preparation 15 minutes • Cooking 20–25 minutes
Difficulty 1

1. Preheat the oven to 325°F (170°C/gas 3). Line a 7 x 11-inch (18 x 28-cm) baking pan with parchment paper. Mix the oats, sunflower seeds, coconut, and flour in a large bowl.
2. Combine the butter and golden syrup in a medium saucepan and stir over low heat until melted. Stir in the sugar, apricots, peanut butter, and vanilla. Pour into the bowl with the dry ingredients and mix until well combined.
3. Spoon into the prepared pan, pressing down firmly with the back of the spoon. Bake for 20-25 minutes, until golden brown. Let cool in the pan on a wire rack. Cut into 18–20 bars and serve.

If you liked this recipe, you will love these as well.

LOW-FAT strawberry shortcake

SEED & NUT bars

FRUIT & NUT bars

GLUTEN- & DAIRY-FREE chocolate mini muffins

- 3/4 cup (120 g) garbanzo bean (chickpea) flour
- 1/4 cup (30 g) potato starch
- 2 tablespoons arrowroot
- 1 cup (200 g) raw sugar
- 2 1/4 teaspoons baking powder
- 1/4 teaspoon baking soda (bicarbonate of soda)
- 1/4 teaspoon xanthan gum
- 1/2 teaspoon salt
- 1/2 cup (75 g) unsweetened cocoa powder
- 1/2 cup (120 g) unsweetened applesauce
- 1/2 cup (120 ml) canola oil
- 2 tablespoons vanilla extract (essence)
- 1/2 cup (120 ml) boiling water
- 2 cups (360 g) vegan gluten-free chocolate chips

Makes 36 • Preparation 15 minutes • Cooking 12–15 minutes
Difficulty 1

1. Preheat the oven to 325°F (170°C/gas 3). Brush 36 mini-muffin pans with oil.
2. Combine the garbanzo bean flour, potato starch, arrowroot, raw sugar, baking powder, baking soda, xanthan gum, salt, and unsweetened cocoa powder in a bowl.
3. Mix the applesauce, oil, and vanilla in a bowl. Slowly add to the flour mixture, stirring to combine. Stir in the water until a batter forms. Fold in the chocolate chips.
4. Put 1 tablespoon of batter in each mini-muffin cup. Bake for 12–15 minutes, until a toothpick inserted into the center comes out clean. Let cool completely on a wire rack.

LOW-FAT banana muffins

- 2 cups (300 g) all-purpose (plain) flour
- 2 teaspoons baking powder
- 1 teaspoon ground cinnamon
- $^1/_2$ teaspoon baking soda (bicarbonate of soda)
- 1 cup (100 g) old-fashioned (quick-cooking) rolled oats
- $^1/_2$ cup (100 g) dark brown sugar
- 2 large eggs
- $^3/_4$ cup (180 ml) plain low-fat yogurt
- $^1/_4$ cup (60 ml) canola oil
- 2 bananas, mashed (about 8 ounces/250 g)

Makes 12 • Preparation 15 minutes • Cooking 20-25 minutes
Difficulty 1

1. Preheat the oven to 400°F (200°C/gas 6). Line a standard 12 cup muffin tin with paper liners. Combine the flour, baking powder, cinnamon, and baking soda in a bowl. Stir in the oats and brown sugar.
2. Whisk the eggs, yogurt, and oil in a medium bowl. Add the bananas and stir to combine. Add to the flour mixture and stir with a wooden spoon until just combined.
3. Spoon the batter evenly into the prepared pans. Bake for 20–25 minutes, until risen and golden brown. Cool for 5 minutes, then transfer to a wire rack and let cool completely.

These applesauce brownies will be a hit with everyone. You can use unsweetened canned applesauce or simply peel and stew a large cooking apple with 2 tablespoons of water until tender, then mash with a fork until smooth.

DIABETIC applesauce brownies

- 1 cup (150 g) all-purpose (plain) flour
- 1 teaspoon baking powder
- $^1/_2$ teaspoon baking soda (bicarbonate of soda)
- $^1/_3$ cup (90 ml) vegetable oil
- $^1/_2$ cup (120 g) unsweetened applesauce
- $^1/_2$ cup (75 g) unsweetened cocoa powder
- $^1/_2$ cup (100 g) sugar
- 2 large eggs, lightly beaten
- 1 teaspoon vanilla extract (essence)
- $^1/_4$ cup (30 g) slivered almonds

Makes 16 • Preparation 15 minutes • Cooking 20–30 minutes
Difficulty 1

1. Preheat the oven to 375°F (190°C/gas 5). Line a 9-inch (23-cm) square pan with parchment paper. Combine the flour, baking powder, and baking soda in a bowl.
2. Combine the oil, applesauce, and cocoa in a bowl. Add the sugar and whisk until dissolved. Beat in the eggs and vanilla, followed by the flour mixture. Spoon the batter into the prepared pan and sprinkle with the almonds.
3. Bake for 20–30 minutes, until a toothpick inserted into the center comes out clean. Let cool in the pan on a wire rack. Cut into squares and serve.

If you liked this recipe, you will love these as well.

GLUTEN-FREE
chocolate roulade

EGG-FREE
cupcakes

GLUTEN- & DAIRY-FREE
chocolate mini muffins

HAZELNUT cookies

- 2 cups (250 g) hazelnuts, toasted and skinned
- 1¼ cups (250 g) sugar
- 4 large egg whites
- ½ teaspoon salt
- 1 teaspoon vanilla extract (essence)

Makes 40–50 • Preparation 30 minutes • Cooking 25–30 minutes
Difficulty 2

1. Preheat the oven to 325°F (170°C/gas 3). Line two baking sheets with parchment paper. Chop the hazelnuts and sugar in a food processor until finely ground. Place in a large bowl.
2. Beat the egg whites and salt in a large bowl with an electric mixer on medium speed until stiff peaks form. Fold the egg whites and vanilla into the nut mixture. Drop tablespoons of the batter onto the prepared baking sheets, spacing 2 inches (5 cm) apart.
3. Bake for 25–30 minutes, until golden brown. Let cool on the baking sheets for 5 minutes. Transfer to a wire rack on the parchment paper and let cool completely.

CHOCOLATE CHIP meringues

- 3 large egg whites
- $^{1}/_{4}$ teaspoon cream of tartar
- $^{3}/_{4}$ cup (150 g) sugar
- $^{1}/_{2}$ teaspoon vanilla extract (essence)
- 3 tablespoons unsweetened cocoa powder
- 1 tablespoon ground cinnamon
- $^{1}/_{2}$ cup (90 g) mini chocolate chips

Makes 30-35 • Preparation 15 minutes • Cooking 1½ hours • Difficulty 1

1. Preheat the oven to 200°F (110°C). Line two large baking sheets with parchment paper.
2. Put the egg whites in a bowl. Add the cream of tartar and beat with an electric mixer on medium speed until soft peaks form. Gradually add the sugar, 1 tablespoon at a time, beating until stiff and glossy. Add the vanilla. Sift in the cocoa and cinnamon and gently fold into the meringue along with the chocolate chips.
3. Fill a pastry bag fitted with a ½-inch (1-cm) plain tip with the meringue. Pipe into 2-inch (5-cm) cookies, spacing 2 inches (5 cm) apart.
4. Bake until crisp and dry, about 1½ hours. Transfer to wire racks on the parchment paper and let cool completely.

CRANBERRY squares

Makes 16–20 • Preparation 15 minutes • Cooking 30–35 minutes • Difficulty 1

- 1 cup (150 g) all-purpose (plain) flour
- 1/2 teaspoon ground cinnamon
- 1/4 cup (60 g) salted butter, melted
- 3/4 cup (150 g) sugar
- 1 large egg, beaten
- 2/3 cup (70 g) finely chopped pecans
- 1 cup (150 g) fresh or frozen cranberries
- 2 tablespoons confectioners' (icing) sugar, to dust

1. Preheat the oven to 350°F (180°C/gas 4). Butter a 9-inch (23-cm) square baking pan. Mix the flour and cinnamon in a medium bowl.
2. Mix the butter and sugar in a medium bowl. Add the egg, beating until just blended. Mix in the dry ingredients, pecans, and cranberries until well blended. Spread the mixture in the prepared pan.
3. Bake for 30–35 minutes, until just golden and a toothpick inserted into the center comes out clean. Cool completely in the pan. Dust with the confectioners' sugar and cut into squares.

NUTTY COFFEE squares

Makes 16 • Preparation 30 minutes • Cooking 35–40 minutes • Difficulty 1

- 1 1/3 cups (200 g) whole almonds
- 2 tablespoons water
- 3/4 cup (150 g) sugar
- 2 teaspoons instant coffee granules
- 2 large egg whites
- 1/4 teaspoon salt
- Confectioners' (icing) sugar, to dust

1. Preheat the oven to 350°F (180°C/gas 4). Butter an 8-inch (20-cm) square baking pan. Place the almonds in a large bowl and pour in enough hot water to cover. Let stand for 5 minutes. Drain and place on a clean cloth. Gently rub to remove the skins. Discard the skins. Finely chop the almonds.
2. Bring the water, sugar, and coffee to a boil in a small saucepan. Stir in the almonds. Set aside.
3. Beat the egg whites and salt in a large bowl with an electric mixer on medium speed until stiff peaks form. Fold into the almond mixture. Spoon into the prepared pan.
4. Bake for 35–40 minutes, until a toothpick inserted into the center comes out clean. Cool in the pan. Dust with confectioners' sugar and cut into squares.

SEED & NUT bars

Make 12 bars • Preparation 20 minutes • Cooking 30–35 minutes • Difficulty 1

- 1/3 cup (90 g) unsalted butter, softened
- 1/3 cup (90 ml) honey
- 1/2 cup (100 g) raw sugar
- 1 1/2 cups (225 g) old-fashioned (quick-cooking) rolled oats
- 1/2 cup (60 g) coarsely chopped walnuts
- 1/2 cup (60 g) raisins
- 2 tablespoons each pumpkin seeds, sunflower seeds, sesame seeds
- 2 tablespoons shredded (desiccated) coconut
- 1 teaspoon ground cinnamon

1. Preheat the oven to 375°F (190°C/gas 5). Butter a 7 x 11-inch (18 x 28-cm) baking pan.
2. Melt the butter with the honey and raw sugar in a medium saucepan over low heat, stirring constantly. Bring to a boil and simmer until the sugar has dissolved completely.
3. Remove from the heat and stir in the oats, walnuts, raisins, pumpkin seeds, sunflower seeds, sesame seeds, coconut, and cinnamon. Spoon the mixture evenly into the prepared pan, smoothing with the back of the spoon.
4. Bake for 30–35 minutes, until just golden. Let cool completely in the pan before cutting into bars.

FRUIT & NUT bars

Make 12 bars • Preparation 15 minutes • Cooking 25–30 minutes • Difficulty 1

- 1 cup (200 g) pitted dates
- 1 1/2 cups (225 g) old-fashioned (quick-cooking) rolled oats
- 1 cup (150 g) pecans, finely chopped
- 1/2 cup (60 g) macadamia nuts, coarsely chopped
- 1/3 cup (60 g) dried papaya, chopped
- 1/3 cup (60 g) dried cherries, chopped
- 1/3 cup (60 g) dried blueberries
- 2 tablespoons oat bran
- 3 tablespoons ground flaxseed
- 2 tablespoons wheat germ
- 1/8 teaspoon coarse salt
- 1/2 teaspoon ground cinnamon
- 3 tablespoons honey

1. Preheat the oven to 350°F (180°C/gas 4). Butter an 8-inch (20-cm) square baking pan. Put the dates in a small saucepan, cover with water, and bring to a boil. Drain well. Chop in a food processor until smooth.
2. Combine the oats, pecans, macadamias, papaya, cherries, blueberries, bran, flaxseed, wheat germ, salt, and cinnamon in a bowl. Mix in the dates and honey. Press into the prepared pan in an even layer.
3. Bake for 20–25 minutes, until firm and golden brown. Cool completely in the pan. Cut into bars with a serrated knife.

GLUTEN-FREE chocolate cookies

- 3 cups (450 g) confectioners' (icing) sugar
- 3/4 cup (120 g) unsweetened cocoa powder
- 1/2 teaspoon salt
- 5 ounces (150 g) unsweetened dark chocolate, chopped
- 1 1/2 cups (180 g) chopped pecans
- 4 large egg whites, lightly beaten

Makes 30–32 • Preparation 15 minutes • Cooking 25–30 minutes
Difficulty 1

1. Preheat the oven to 325°F (170°C/gas 3). Line two large baking sheets with parchment paper.
2. Combine the confectioners' sugar, cocoa, and salt in a large bowl. Stir in the chocolate and pecans. Add the egg whites and stir until just combined; do not overmix.
3. Drop heaped tablespoons of the dough onto the prepared baking sheets, spacing about 3 inches (8-cm) apart. Bake for 25–30 minutes, until the cookies are dry and cracked.
4. Transfer the sheets to wire racks and let cool completely.

GLUTEN-FREE almond shortbread

- $^1/_3$ cup (90 g) unsalted butter, softened
- $^1/_2$ cup (100 g) sugar
- Seeds from $^1/_2$ vanilla bean
- 1 cup (150 g) brown rice flour
- 1 cup (150 g) finely ground almonds
- $^1/_2$ teaspoon salt

Makes 16 • Preparation 15 minutes + 30 minutes to freeze • Cooking 45–55 minutes • Difficulty 1

1. Line an 8-inch (20-cm) square baking pan with parchment, leaving a 2-inch (5-cm) overhang on two sides.
2. Beat the butter, sugar, and vanilla seeds in a bowl with an electric mixer on medium speed until pale and creamy. With the mixer on low speed, add the brown rice flour, almonds, and salt, beating until just combined.
3. Press the dough into the prepared pan and freeze until firm, 30 minutes. Preheat the oven to 350°F (180°C/gas 4).
4. Score the shortbread into 16 pieces. Bake for 45–55 minutes, until golden brown. Let cool for 15 minutes, then unmold using the overhanging parchment. Let cool on a wire rack. Cut into pieces along the scorelines to serve.

INDEX